A Message of Reason and Virtue

Daniel L. Abraham

A Message of Reason and Virtue

Medlogic Research, Inc.
New York, USA

Library of Congress
Control Number
2016921222

ISBN-13: 978-0-9985568-0-2 Paperback
ISBN-13: 978-0-692-77513-4 eBook

Printed in USA

Preface

Reason is thinking rationally. Conscience in action is called virtue; moral excellence. The key message of the Quran, scripture of Islam is to reason, reflect on life and exercise faith through the works of virtue. It is a message for all of the humanity to honor their Creator and serve each other. It focuses on the big questions of life: "Who made us? "Why are we here?" and "How should we behave?"

This book is dedicated to the curious minds so that they can understand this message and know basics of Islam. Chapters of the book include Abraham's faith, people of the Bible, interfaith commandments, human rights, and social justice to identify our shared values and ethics. Such basic knowledge is crucial for mutual understanding and harmonious coexistence.

Let us unite on common principles and accept our differences. Let us work together for peace and common good and lead a purposeful life. We all pray to our Creator, for guidance, mercy, and blessings. Amen

Who is the author?

The author is a physician who writes under the pen name Daniel L. Abraham. He has studied biomedical sciences, philosophy, and comparative religion to find out the purpose of life. His pen name was inspired by Prophet Abraham who modeled reason-based faith and the name Daniel which means: God is my judge. The middle initial "L." stands for liberty and free will.

Life Motto

*"Live by **reason** and **virtue,** trust in the Lord, and do what is best."*

"...Whoever saves a life; saves all of humankind..."

A dollar can save a life.

The royalty of this work is primarily going to charity.

Acknowledgements

Praise is due to God for empowering me with the knowledge and resources to write this book. Thanks to my beloved family and friends who encouraged me and reviewed the script. Acknowledgments to Imam Nazim Mangera, Dr. Khalid Qazi, Professor Faizan Haq, Richard Polley, Amber Shaikh, Cassandra Williams, Esq., Imam Muhammed Agwa, Ph.D., and Joanna Fogarassi. Eng. Nancy Farouk, nancy@colors-me.com designed the book cover. God bless everyone who helped and supported me through this endeavor.

Contents

What is Islam?

- Islam takes its name from the Arabic word "Salam" meaning; 1) making something safe and secure, 2) making something sound and whole, 3) entering into peace and tranquility 4) submission and obedience to God. The name of the religion embodies its underlying message. A way of life symbolized by peace, security and a purposeful lifestyle. It is peace within oneself and peace with the creations of God through submission to God and commitment to His guidance. A follower of Islam is called a Muslim. The word "Islamic" refers to doctrines and practices derived from Islam. (1)

- Traditional vs. Universal Islam: The word "Islam" is used primarily to refer to the doctrines and teachings of the prophet Muhammad which dates back to the 7th century CE; this is the traditional sense of the word. At the same time, the Quran, the holy book of Islam, teaches the universal sense of the word; Islam existed since Adam and Eve and was the path taught by all the prophets of God including Noah, Abraham, Moses, David, Jesus, and Muhammad.

- Islam vs. Muslims: Islam is not the same as Muslims. Islam is a way of living and code of ethics as portrayed in the Quran. Islam is a moral law and practiced religion. "Muslims" is a descriptive term for the people who aspire to follow the tenets of Islam. Their actions may not comply with Islam. Some Muslims' actions represent their local customs and cultures, not Islam. (1)

- The terms Muslim and Arab are not synonymous: Islam is a global faith. Arabs are the ethnic groups united by the Arabic language. About 20 % of Muslims are Arabs. The global Muslim population is 22.74% as per the World Fact Book 2010. Although many Arabs are Muslims, a considerable minority of Arabs are Christians of various denominations. Muslims include a vast range of races, nationalities, and cultures from around the globe. The world's largest Muslim community is in Indonesia. Substantial parts of Asia are Muslims, while significant minorities live in India, China, Russia, North and South America, Eastern and Western Europe. (1)

- The term Muhammadan is a misnomer of Muslim: Some Europeans use the term to refer to Muslims as followers of Muhammad. In Islam, Prophet Muhammad is a human being and not divine. Muslims adore and emulate him, but it is only God that Muslims worship. Prophet Muhammad is merely the messenger and servant of God. (1)

What is the Quran?

The Quran defines itself as the revelation from the Creator of the universe to His prophet, Muhammad, providing guidance to all of the humanity. The Quran, which literally means reading, was revealed to Muhammad over the course of his prophetic period, through Gabriel, the archangel of revelations. Prophet Muhammad delivered the Quran orally, in Arabic, and appointed scribes to write it down. The early followers of Islam eagerly memorized and recorded each revelation. The Quran took a textual form during Muhammad's lifetime and, by the time of his death; thousands had memorized the entire Quran by heart. (2)

The Quran is the guide for whoever wonders about the purpose of life and their existence. The Quran addresses a number of central topics: 1) God's supreme power and authority, 2) the accountability of individual human beings for their actions, 3) natural life and human behavior, 4) stories of the prophets and their peoples, 5) descriptions of Judgment Day and the afterlife, and 6) doctrinal tenets and moral commands. (3) The Quran provides guidelines for a just society, proper human conduct and fair economic principles. The various parts of the Quran span multiple literary genres and techniques, including symbolic and historical narratives, moral injunctions, prayers, logical arguments, critical thinking questions, parables and metaphors, oaths, and vivid descriptions. (2)

Language and Style

The Quran is written in rhythmic Arabic prose with assonances (similarities in words and syllables) that cannot be replicated in translation. The authorial voice in the Quran is always God's; whether expressed as "I," "We," or "He." Verses that begin with "Say" generally introduce doctrinal maxims (general truths or fundamental principles) and are addressed to Muhammad or believers at large. The intended audience is alternately Muhammad, his family, the believers, the Israelites, the Christians or humankind collectively. The Quran's narrative style is largely nonlinear and often shifts themes or repeats certain ideas, as in a refrain. The Quran is an oral text to be recited as well as a book to be read. The Quran is divided into 114 chapters, each of which consists of numbered verses called signs. The chapters are arranged not in chronological order of their revelation but rather in order of length, from longest to shortest. The beginning of each chapter is marked, both textually and in recitation, with the phrase: "In the name of God, the Compassionate, the Merciful." Often, the title of a chapter reflects the main subject or a keyword in the chapter. (2)

Most translations of the Quran to English have a side-by-side Arabic text and follow the verse and chapter structure of the original. Additionally, translations often provide a commentary, an index, and a table of translated Arabic names. They usually contain parenthetical phrases to elucidate the meaning of the text due to the compact nature of Arabic where a single word can sometimes express an entire sentence. (4) Readers of the Quran translations should be aware that the translated Quran cannot be regarded as presenting the perfection of the original Arabic text. Any translation is qualified only as a translation of the meanings and involves some degree of interpretation. No language, especially Arabic, can be translated with complete accuracy into a foreign tongue.

Revelation and Compilation

The Quran was delivered to Prophet Muhammad as an inspired speech, piecemeal, over twenty-three years. Revelations continued until his death in 632 CE, by which time he had gained thousands of followers. The first Caliph, Abu Bakr requested the prophet's companions who had memorized the entire Quran to collect all existing copies and fragments of the Quran in one place to compile the standard edition. (2)

This manuscript became the basis for the authorized copies that were distributed to each Muslim province during the rule of the third Caliph, Othman (644-656 CE). Remarkably, a few of those early manuscripts have been preserved and can still be viewed in museums today. (5) That is the authoritative Othman edition of the Quran that all Muslims still read today.

Relation to the Bible

The Quran presents itself as being sent from the same God as that of the Bible. It reiterates many of the same moral themes and prophetic narratives and affirms the divine nature of the earlier revelations, particularly those given to Moses, David, and Jesus. The main contention of the Quran regarding these earlier scriptures is that they have been altered over time to the extent that they no longer fully reflect the prophets' original teachings. (2)

The purpose of the revelation to Muhammad is to confirm some of that which was revealed before and to clarify other aspects. Notably, the Quran affirms the monotheism of Abraham and that the Messiah is Jesus and challenges the idea of God as a Trinity. The Quran rejects the concept of salvation or special privilege based on ethnicity. God does not discriminate by race or color. It also denies the need for the sacrifice of an innocent life as a whole or body part for people to attain salvation or honor the covenant. (2)

The Quran describes the original scriptures of Torah and Gospel as light and guidance. The Quran has a significant legalistic component reminiscent of the Old Testament book of Leviticus, and poetic content as beautifully uplifting as the book of Psalms. Like the

Bible, it is common practice to cite the number of its chapter and verse(s). However, the Quran does not follow a historical timeline. (2)

The Quran is Unique

The Quran presents itself as the culmination of a series of divine books. These started with the messages revealed to Adam, regarded in Islam as the first prophet, and continued with the Scrolls of Abraham, the Torah, the Psalms, and the Gospel. The Quran includes major narratives mentioned in Jewish and Christian scriptures, summarizing some, dwelling at length on others, and, in some cases, presenting alternative accounts and interpretations of events. (6)

- The Quran is recited in the daily prayer, particularly the first chapter, the opening. Reading and reciting the Quran is a form of meditative devotion. Observant Muslims honor God by studying the Quran and living by its teachings.

- The Quran also enters devotional life through the art of calligraphy, which adorns many books, Art Works, and mosques.

- The Quran has been memorized in entirety by millions of people through generations, of all ages, social ranks, and intellectual abilities, including non-Arabic speakers.

- Learning Arabic as a second language to understand Quran has a beneficial impact on Muslims lives. Diverse cultures and ethnic groups have been able to communicate through Arabic as a second language.

- Learning a second language enhances brain activity and mental fitness. (7) That benefit extends to non-Arab speakers who study the Quran and learn basics of Islam.

- Arabic is a living language. So, the Quran is preserved in its original language. The Quran has no versions or editions. There have never been additions or revisions.

God's Message

The Quran presents itself as God's living miracle to all humankind and admonishes them that they are accountable before God on the Day of Judgment: *"Whoever has done an atom's weight of good will see it. And whoever has done an atom's weight of evil will see it"* (Quran 99:7-8).

The Quran challenges everyone who has doubt in it to produce a chapter like any of its chapters: *"Should you have any doubt about what We have revealed to our servant, bring one chapter comparable to it and call your witnesses before God if your claim is true. If you do not produce such a chapter, and you will never do so, then guard yourselves against fire, whose fuel will be people and stones, already set up for those who reject the truth" (Quran2:23-24).*

The Quran gives glad tidings to whoever exercises faith through the works of virtue: *"And give glad tidings to those who believe and do righteous deeds that they will have gardens, under which rivers flow (Paradise). Every time they are fed with fruits, they say: 'This is what we got before.' And they shall be given similar items. They shall have pure spouses and abide therein (forever)"* (Quran 2:25).

Life Reasoning

As portrayed in the Quran, Islam is a reason-based faith. Islam encourages inquiry and counsels its followers to study, search and investigate. Everyone should use reasoning faculties to obtain knowledge and attain truth. (8) God has given every human the conscience as a personal monitor and the reason as a guide to living. There is an impulse in everyone to seek understanding and knowledge. The fundamental motivation of knowledge is the deep curiosity about the nature of the world and discovery of truth: *"Say, walk in the earth; and see how creation started"* (Quran 29:20).

Human beings are commanded by the Quran to have critical thinking, reasoning and provide the proof for arguments and evidence for claims: *"Have they not looked at the camels, how they are created and the sky, how it is raised up and the mountains, how they are installed and the earth, how it is spread out. So keep on preaching, you are only a preacher"* (Quran 88:17-21). Islam is an evidence-based religion: *"Say: Bring your proof if you are truthful"* (Quran 2:111). The Quran emphasizes reason as essential to life, and that humans are created as both intellectual and moral beings: *"God reveals signs and lessons and admonition so that you may think"* (Quran 59:21).

The Quran gives the answers to the main questions of life: Where do we come from? What is the purpose of life? What is the death like? Is there life, after death? Do Paradise and Hell exist? What is the origin of life? Who is our Creator? What does the Creator demand from us? Why is the humankind created? Do humans have a choice? Why are there suffering and adversity? Why is there good and evil? How can we discern between right and wrong? How should we behave? (9)

God created humans with a life span divided into two periods: the earthly life, and the afterlife. Earthly life is merely a test, determining one's eternal afterlife, either in Paradise or Hell. The Quran reminds us that earthly life is temporary and just a time-share. Earthly life is our only opportunity to come to terms with God. The afterlife is the time for receiving the reward or punishment merited by one's faith and actions. The message of the Quran is to make humans aware of this reality and guide them on what to do. (2)

Quran describes the purpose of life as follows: *"Blessed be He in Whose Hand is the kingdom, He is powerful over all things, Who created death and life that He might examine which of you is best in deeds, and He is the Almighty, the Forgiving"* (Quran 67:1-2). The purpose of life is to honor God and service His creations as guided by the Quran, *"And I created not the jinn and humankind except that they should worship Me"* (Quran 51:56). *"Then, We made you [people] vicegerents [deputy] so that We know how you would act"* (Quran 10:14).

The Earth is a living planet where many complex systems run perfectly and continuously, without pause. It is specially designed for life, when compared to other planets. Life prevails in every spot of this unique planet, from the atmosphere to the depths of the earth. We wonder how a tree grows from an acorn, how flower blooms and how DNA can shape the appearance and character of a living creature. It is miraculous how life is based on delicate balances and water. It is marvelous how the earth is placed in our Milky Way galaxy which contains billions of stars similar to our sun. At the molecular level, we wonder how the atom functions as a collection of remarkable components (matter and antimatter) rotating in different directions, yet held together by immense power.

Studying molecular biology and reasoning the awesome complexity and diversity of life processes leads to the conclusion that life could not have arisen by chance. It is the intelligent design created by God. God is the Originator and Sustainer of the universe, *"Assuredly in the creation of Heavens and of the Earth; and in the alternation of night and day; and in the ships which sail through the sea with what benefits humankind; and in the rain allowed to fall for the parched land to live and in the diversity of living creatures; and in the change of the winds, and in the changing patterns of winds and clouds that service between the heavens and the earth are signs for those who understand"* (Quran 2:164).

The Quran envisions death as a natural and inevitable stage of life. Death is nothing to fear. All living creatures are mortal. After death, their bodies are recycled to the environment, and souls return to the Creator. Humans reflect on life and realize that none of their successes, fame, or wealth will save them from growing old and dying. Some people reflect on suffering and adversity and view life as a haphazard and injustice. Such thought brings despair to those who see no ultimate purpose in life. Believers view suffering and adversity as tests from God and problems as learning opportunities. They remain steadfast against evil and strive for the good. They put their trust in God and do their best.

The creation of a human in the mother's womb is a miracle. The sperm unites with the ovum to form a living cell. Then this cell multiplies. The multiplying cells differentiate by a secret order. They are arranged and integrated to form the bones, eyes, heart, lungs brain, liver, skin, etc. At the end of this complex process, a single cell turns into a perfect human being with about ten trillion cells. God calls out to humankind to reflect on this creation: *"O Human! What has deluded you in respect of your Noble Lord? Who created you and formed you and proportioned you and assembled you in whatever way He willed"* (Quran 82:6-8).

The Quran uses the first creation of human beings, the fact that every individual has been brought to the world to show that what happened once can happen again. God is All-Mighty, Who originated the creation (Quran 29:19). The Quran alludes to the fact that the phenomenon of resurrection is foreshadowed in this world: *"It is He Who sends the winds as heralds of glad tidings, going before His mercy: when they have carried the heavy-laden clouds, We drive them to a land that is dead make rain descend thereon, and produce every kind of harvest therewith: Thus We raise up the dead…"* (Quran 7:57).

The Quran reasons human existence, the purpose of life and the arguments of unbelievers: *"They say: There is nothing but our existence in the world. We die, and we live, and nothing destroys us except for time. They have no knowledge of that. They are only conjecturing"* (Quran 45: 24). *"Do they not think about themselves: God did not create the heavens and the earth and what is between them but for a just cause, and for a set time? Many people are deniers of the meeting with their Lord"* (Quran 30:8).

The Quran reasons with those who question creation and life after death stating, *"He has set up an argument and forgot his creation. He said, 'Who will give life to the bones when they are decayed?' Say, 'These will be revived by the same One who had created them for the first time, and Who is fully aware of every creation; the One who created for you fire from the green tree, so you kindle from it.' Is it that the One who has created the heavens and the earth has no power to create ones like them? Why not? He is the Supreme Creator, the All-Knowing. His practice, when He intends to do something, is no more than He says, 'be!' and it comes to be. So, pure and exalted is the One in whose hand is the dominion of all things. And towards Him you are to be returned"* (Quran 36:78-83).

The Quran proclaims that humankind has dominated everything in the Heavens and the Earth. Humans are the highest creation of God. The creator gives them knowledge and freedom. Every human being has free will, action, and choice. (Quran 18:29) Consequently, he/she is responsible for his/her acts and will be accountable before God on the Day of Judgment. Those who have faith and do good deeds shall go to the Paradise. On the other hand, those who reject faith and do evil shall go to the Hell: *"There is no doubt that evil doers who are engulfed in sins are the companions of Hellfire wherein they will live forever. As for the righteously striving believers, they will be among the people of Paradise wherein they will live forever"* (Quran 2: 81-2).

God created Adam to place him on the earth for a positive exemplary role as vicegerent. God endowed human beings with free will that enables each person despite hereditary and or environment to choose to do good or evil. The angels exclaimed that Adam could be a vicegerent, despite the potential that he could spread corruption and shed blood, while the angels' role would be to glorify and praise God. (10) God gave Adam the power of knowledge. He demonstrated to the angels Adam's ability and ordered them to bow to Adam in respect (Quran 2:30-34). The angels all bowed except for Satan. When Satan was questioned about why he did not bow to Adam, he stated: *"...I am better than him. You created me from fire and created him from clay"* (Quran 38:76). After that, God banished Satan and the jinni that followed him.

Satan declared that he would mislead all humans, except for the sincere servants of God, away from the right path, into err and disbelief. Satan has no authority over humankind other than whispering. Satan was cursed because of his disobedience and arrogance. Satan is the real enemy of humanity and the role model of racism and arrogance. The Quran says that the root of evil is not always material wants, money, or greed. Often the heart of evil is arrogance, key elements of which are putting self above all others, assigning to oneself special priority and neglecting the rights of others. (11)

Who is Allah?

Allah is the standard Arabic name for God. Allah means the same as the words "Dieu" in French, "Gott" in German and "Dios" in Spanish. The word Allah is used by Arabic-speakers including Jews and Christians referencing to God. The term was also used by pagan Arabs referencing to the Creator God. If you pick up an Arabic Bible, you will see the word Allah being used where God is used in English. Allah is the Arabic equivalent of Elohim and Yahweh, the Hebrew names of God and "Elah" the Aramaic name of God as the awesome one. (12) The word Allah has no plural or gender compared to the word God. Allah is not the personal name of a deity within a pantheon.

Allah is the proper name of God. He is the sole deity, Lord of the universe. In Islamic tradition, God is named by His divine attributes, for example, the Merciful, the Compassionate, the Truthful, the Loving, the Sustainer, the Creator, and the Just. There are about ninety-nine "best names" or attributes of God in Islam, all of which refer to God, the Supreme, and All-Comprehensive divine names: *"God, there is no deity but He. To Him belong the best names"* (Quran 20:8).

Allah is the one God, beyond imagination, the Creator of all. God is neither begetting nor begotten (neither born nor procreates). God transcends time and space. God is the Creator of everything and the Guardian over everything. Worship testifies to the oneness of God in His Lordship, His names, and His attributes: *"Say: He is God, the One. God, the Eternal. He begets not, nor is He begotten. And none is like Him"* (Quran 112:1-4). *"The Creator of the heavens and the earth; He made mates for you from among yourselves, and mates of the cattle too, multiplying you thereby; nothing is like Him; and He is the All-Hearing, the All-Seeing"* (Quran 42:11).

God is the Creator, Sustainer, and Sovereign of the universe: *"He is God; there is no deity but He. He is the Knower of the unseen and the visible; He is the Merciful, the Compassionate. He is God; there is no deity but He. He is the King, the Holy, the All-Peace, the Guardian of the Faith, the All-Preserver, the Almighty, the One Who subdues wrong and restores right, the Exalted One. Glory be to God, above that they ascribe a share in His divinity! He is God, the Creator, the Maker, the Shaper. To Him belong the Most Beautiful Names. All that is in the heavens and the earth glorifies Him; He alone is the Almighty, truly Wise"* (Quran 59:22-24).

The Quran answers the question "Who is God?" by stating, "*...Who originates the creation, then reproduces it and Who gives you sustenance from the heaven and the earth. Is there a deity With God? Say: Bring your proof if you are* *truthful"* (Quran 27:64). The Quran informs us that God breathed something of His spirit into every human soul (Quran 32:9). The virtues that humans experience are but a breath of the God's best names. God is the infinite source of all love, mercy, kindness and wisdom that we experience and feel. (11) Ritual Prayer is the link between the believer and God. The believer feels God's love and mercy through prayer.

God is the basis of morality and ethics; by what authority can anyone argue that certain activities should be permitted and others forbidden? Different individuals have different conceptions of what is moral or even if being moral is desired. Who would choose desire (ego) over God? The concept of morality without God is an illusion. Simply if there is no God, everything is permitted: *"Have you seen a person who takes his desire as his god?! Would you be his guardian?"* (Quran 25:43).

God is portrayed in the Quran as follows: *"God is the Light of the heavens and the earth. The example of His Light is that of a niche and within it a Lamp: the Lamp enclosed in glass- the glass looks like a brilliant planet: Lit from a blessed tree, an olive, which is neither eastern nor western. Its oil is about to emit light even though the fire has not touched it. Light upon Light. God guides to His light whomever He wills; God describes examples for the people, God is All-Knowing of everything"* (Quran 24:35).

In God We Trust

The core of monotheism is that there is no deity but God and that all else is God's creation. The primary covenant was made between God and all human souls that God is the Lord of all. The word "Kufr" is the Arabic word of unbelief. It literally means covering up the truth. It indicates the refusal to be guided by one's conscience, by signs of God or by God's messengers.

The Arabic word "Shirk" means idolatry or polytheism. It refers to faith in a deity other than God, or faith in multiple deities, whether they are objects, persons or concepts. The Arabic word "taqwa" means fear, reverence, and conscience of God. The Arabic word "tawakkul" means trust in and reliance upon God. The Quran teaches that we must turn to God and put our trust in Him. God Almighty, our Creator, always keeps promises and always remains in control.

Observant Muslims put hope in God and use the Arabic phrase "Insha' Allah" (meaning "God willing") after references to future events. They encourage beginning things with the invocation of "Bism-Allah"(meaning "In the name of God"). They use "Subhan-Allah" (holiness be to God), "Alhamdul-Allah" (Praise be to God), "La-Illaha-Illa-Allah" (There is no deity but God) and "Allahu Akbar" (God is greater) as spiritual devotional exercises.

God is greater is an unfinished comparative. God is greater affirms that He is incomparably greater. He is greater than any likening we may use to complete this declaration. God is greater than anything or everything that we could ever conceive. God is greater than the speculations of theologians or the assertions of dogmatists or the formulations of philosophers. God is greater than human words can describe. (10)

God is indefinitely greater, is the key Muslim perception of God. It is the reason for worship, total trust in and submission to Him. It allows for all our praises and glorifications. If God is indefinitely greater, why should one seek other deities or intermediary between oneself and God? Why should one seek another ultimate goal or protector? For Muslims, the answer is obvious: there is no deity, but God and therefore, worship is due to God alone. (10)

Trust in God is the guiding principle in Islam: "Say: He (God) is the Gracious: We have believed in Him, and in Him we trust…" (Quran 67:29). "Put your trust in God. God loves those who trust [in Him]" (Quran 3:159). "And unto God belongs all that is in the heavens and all that is on earth, and none is as worthy of trust as God" (Quran 4:132).

Who is Muhammad?

Prophet Muhammad (peace be upon him) came to revive the message of the first commandment preached by Moses and Jesus concerning the belief in one God. His message is to call all of the humankind to the monotheism of Abraham. He is the role model for Muslims to aspire to and was an active preacher, reformer, and leader, who opposed ignorance and injustice. His name means highly praised, and his message is based on Mercy: *"And We did not send you but as a mercy to all worlds"* (Quran 21:107).

Prophet Muhammad was born in Mecca in the year 570 (C.E.), during the period of history Europeans call the middle ages. Since his father died before his birth and his mother shortly afterward, he was raised by his uncle. As he grew up, he became known for his truthfulness, generosity, sincerity and good work ethics, so he earned the titles the "truthful" and the "trustworthy" one. He first worked as a shepherd then as a merchant. At the age of twenty-five, he married a widow called Khadija who had employed him as a manager of her trade.

Prophet Muhammad was of a contemplative nature and had long detested the decadence of the pagan society. At the age of 40, he received his first revelation from God through the Archangel Gabriel while engaged in a meditative retreat. These revelations continued for twenty-three years and are known as the Quran. Afterward, he began preaching publicly and called his people to worship God, amend their behavior and share the wealth with the poor. He and his small group of followers suffered bitter persecution and boycott, which grew so fierce that some Muslims had to immigrate to Abyssinia (Currently Ethiopia).

The pagan tribes of Mecca did not allow freedom of religion. They oppressed believers in God and imposed worship of idols. Violence, indecency, exploitation, and abuse of power were prevalent. Prophet Muhammad and his followers had to emigrate from Mecca to Medina where they found support and refuge. In Medina, he founded his mosque and led the Medina community.

Prophet Muhammad drafted the city charter (constitution) spelling out the rights and responsibilities of all resident groups: 1) All citizens shall live in peace and be secure, 2) No side shall make alliances with an enemy of any party, and 3) Economic rights and religious freedom are to be respected. This charter was the foundation of a pluralistic society with freedom and justice for all. Prophet Muhammad emphasized the golden rule in his tradition: *"None of you (truly) believes until he wishes for his brother what he wishes for himself."*

However, the unbelievers from Mecca went after him to invade Medina and launched wars against him and his followers. Prophet Muhammad has had to defend himself, his family and his followers from being slain, crucified or enslaved. After several battles including a siege of Medina, he was successful in securing Medina and then Mecca.

After the victory, Prophet Muhammad gave a general amnesty to those who fought against him. Before the Prophet died at the age of sixty-three, the greater part of Arabia was Muslim, and within a century of his death, Islam had spread to Spain, to the West, and as far East as China. The life of Prophet Muhammed was a tireless campaign against greed, injustice, and arrogance. (13)

Prophet Muhammad was viewed as the greatest influential person in history by the American writer, Michael Hart who stated: "My choice of Muhammad to lead the list of the world's most influential persons may surprise some readers and may be questioned by others, but he was the only man in history who was supremely successful on both the religious and secular level." (14)

The British writer, Thomas Carlyle was amazed by the leadership of Prophet Muhammad "How one man single-handedly, could weld warring tribes and wandering Bedouins into a most powerful and civilized nation in two decades?" (15) This nation is viewed as one of the God's promises to Abraham: *"Yet I will also make a nation of the son of the bondwoman, because he is your seed"* (Genesis 21:13).

Prophet Muhammad preached the faith of Abraham and called on monotheism and reformation of religious practices. All human beings are equal before God, Who will judge them on their merits alone. *"Then We revealed to you (O Muhammad): Follow the faith of Abraham, the upstanding, who was not one of the polytheist"* (Quran 16:123).

A Message for All

The Quran addresses all of the humanity to worship God, the Creator of the universe and challenges those who are in doubt to bring a similitude of its verses. The Quran calls all humankind to reflect on its verses and their lives. It proclaims that its message is simply a reminder of truths. God commands believers to share faith and declares: *"Call others to the way of your Lord with wisdom and good advice. Reason with them in the best manner. Certainly, your Lord knows who has strayed from His Path and who is guided"* (Quran 16:125).

God raised in every nation a messenger to reform his community. Muslims believe that God sent to all of the humanity prophets, *"…of the seed of Adam, and of those carried with Noah, and of the seed of Abraham and Israel and of those whom we guided and chose"* (Quran 19:58-60). Therefore, God sent prophets to China, India, and other peoples. The religion taught by all the prophets worldwide consisted of four principles:

1) God is relevant to His creation. God as a creator, is our reason for being, gives the purpose of our life and norms and ethics by which everyone lives.

2) God, the Creator of the universe, transcends over all creatures. God has the power and dominion over everything and everyone.

3) Humans are capable of fulfilling the divine imperatives as they know and have free will, guided by conscience and reasoning. God has made nature subservient to humans.

4) Humans are responsible for their actions. Humans are subject to judgment and reward in the case of compliance and punishment in the case of defiance or violation.

The Quran addresses humankind as follows: *"O Humankind, worship your Lord Who created you and those who lived before you so that you may become pious."* (Quran 2:20) *"Children of Adam, did not We command you not to worship Satan? He was your sworn enemy. Did We not command you to worship Me, and tell you that this is the straight path?"* (Quran 36: 60-61). *"O Humankind! Surely the promise of God is true, therefore let not the life of this world deceive you, and let not the arch deceiver (Satan) trick you respecting God"* (Quran 35:5).

The Quran calls humankind to reason about creation by stating: *"O Humankind, an example has been set, so listen to it. Those whom you call upon besides God are not even able to create a single fly even if they were to join to do it. Moreover, if a fly takes something from them, they cannot get it back. How feeble are both the seeker and the sought! They do not appreciate God as it should. God is All-Powerful, Almighty"* (Quran 22: 73-4).

The Quran addresses atheists and agnostics: *"And they say: What! When we shall have become bones and decayed particles, shall we then certainly be raised up, being a new creation? Say: Be you stones or iron; or some other creature of those which are greater in your minds! However, they will say: Who will return us? Say: Whoever created you the first time. Still, they will shake their heads at you and say: When will it be? Say: Maybe it will be soon; On the day when He will call you forth, then you shall obey Him, giving Him praise, and you will think that you stayed but a little while"* (Quran 17:49-52).

The Quran reasons with polytheists and pagans about objects of worship: *"Certainly, those whom you call on before God are servants like you. Call upon them and let them hear your prayer if what your claim is true."* (Quran 7:194) *"So did you think that We created you for nothing and that you will not be returned to Us? So exalted be God, the True King; no deity but He, the Lord of the Noble dominion. And whoever invokes with God another deity while he has no proof for it, his reckoning is only with his Lord; surely the unbelievers will not succeed"* (Quran 23:115-117).

The Quran addresses the Jewish people: *"O children of Israel! Remember My favors to you; fulfill your covenant with Me and I will fulfill My covenant with you.*

And you should fear none but Me. Believe in My revelation (the Quran), which is confirming your scriptures; do not be the first one to deny My revelation, and do not sell them for a small price, fear Me and Me alone. Do not mix the truth with falsehood, or knowingly conceal the truth" (Quran 2:40-42).

The Quran calls the Christians of all denominations to honor the first Commandment, *"O people of the Bible, Do not exaggerate in your religion and do not say anything about God but the truth. The Messiah, Jesus son of Mary is only a messenger of God and His word that He delivered to Mary and a spirit from Him; believe therefore in God and His messengers, and do not say, Trinity. Stop! It is better for you; God is only one Deity. Glory be to Him that He should have a son…"* (Quran 4:171). Believers are commanded not to take angels or prophets as lords before God (Quran 3:80).

The Quran assures that all humans shall be tested including the believers: *"Do humans think that they will be left alone on saying, we believe, and not be tested? Lo! We tested those who were before them. Thus God knows those who are truthful and knows the liars"* (Quran 29:1-2). The Quran reassures believers in God, *"Any believer, male or female, who acts righteously, will enter Paradise and will not suffer the least bit of injustice"* (Quran 4: 124). *"Whoever wants to meet his Lord, He should do good deeds and not associate partners [anyone or anything] with God"* (Quran 18:110).

The Quran teaches that all human beings will be held accountable, on the Day of Judgment, for their beliefs and actions. All of one's deeds will be questioned, and God, Himself, will evaluate the events of one's life. There is no original sin; everyone is responsible for his/her acts only: *"We have made every person's actions cling to his neck. On the Day of Judgment, We will bring forth the record of his actions in the form of a wide open book. We will tell him: read it and judge for yourself. One who follows guidance does so for self, and one who goes astray does so to his soul. No one will suffer for the sins of others. We have never punished anyone without sending them Our Messenger first"* (Quran 17:13-15).

Abraham's Faith

Many of the early civilizations believed in a plurality of gods. This concept was widespread from the temples of ancient Iraq, Syria, Egypt, Greece, Rome, India, and China. The majority of early civilizations worshiped a pantheon of gods, with each deity controlling a sector of the universe. A greater deity governs all of them. Early people practiced idolatry by worshiping statues, idols the physical representations of gods. (16)

In such societies, the pharaoh, emperor, Caesar, or king was generally regarded as divine, a son of God. The priestly class that supported his function was privileged as semi-divine. The society was stratified, the royal and noble classes, the priestly class, the warrior class, the merchant and farming classes. The slaves were ordained to do the most menial and undesirable work. Rejecting the state religion was regarded as treason against the state and violation of the structure of the society, an act punishable by death. The free thinker had to exercise freedom of human conscience outside such society and live as a hermit in a cave. (16)

A man called Abraham was born in a town in ancient Iraq. He found the idea of polytheism nonsense. Biblical and Islamic traditions inform us that Abraham's father was a sculptor of such idols. The young boy Abraham saw his father fabricating such statues from the raw material of wood or stone. Abraham probably realized the concept of the Chinese proverb "He who carves the Buddha never worships him" when he observed the creature creating the creator. (16)

The Quran narrates Abraham's search for truth and reflection on life: *"When the night covered him over with darkness he (Abraham) saw a planet. He said: 'This is my Lord.' However, when it set, he said: 'I like not those that set.' When he saw the moon rising, he said: 'This is my Lord.' However, when it set, he said: 'Unless my Lord guides me, I shall surely be among the erring people.' When he saw the sun rising, he said: 'This is my Lord. This is greater.' However, when it set, he said: 'O my people! I am indeed free from all that you join as partners in worship with God.' Verily, I have turned my face towards God Who has created the heavens and the earth worshipping none but God Alone and I am not of the Idolaters"* (Quran 6: 75-79).

The Quran quotes Abraham as debating: *"Do you worship that which you yourselves sculpt—while God has created you and what you are making?"* (Quran 37:95-96). Abraham argued with his people after smashing the idols: "They said: *'Are you the one who has done this to our gods, O Abraham?' He said: 'Nay, this one, the biggest of them (idols) did it. Ask them, if they can speak!' So they turned to themselves and said: 'Verily, you are the wrongdoer.' Then they turned to themselves. 'Indeed you (Abraham) know well that these (idols) speak not!' (Abraham) said: 'Do you then worship things before God that can neither benefit you nor harm you? Fie on you and what you worship instead of God! Will not you reason?'"* (Quran 21: 59-67).

Abraham used common sense to reason with polytheists as well as with the people who proclaimed themselves as gods. For example, when a king proclaimed himself God, he is disproven as follows: *"Have you not thought about him who disputed with Abraham about his Lord, because God had given him the kingdom? Then, Abraham said (to him): "My Lord is He Who gives life and causes death." He said: "I give life and cause death." Abraham said: "Verily! God causes the sun to rise from the east; would you cause it to rise from the west?" So the disbeliever was utterly defeated. And God guides not the people who are wrongdoers"* (Quran 2: 258).

Abraham clarified who God is to his people saying: *The Lord of all worlds; He who has created me; it is He who guides me; and it is He who feeds me and gives me a drink. And when I am sick, it is He who cures me; and who will cause me to die and then will bring me to life; and who, I hope will forgive me my sins on the Day of Judgment (Quran 26: 69-82).*

Abraham's faith is both reason-based and conscience-guided. So it is the natural faith model for all humankind. After a spiritual search, Abraham reasoned that God is one, the Creator of the universe including celestial bodies and humankind. His reasoning and conscience led him to conclude that worshipping idols that cannot benefit or harm is nonsense. Those who follow Abraham's faith model were known as "Hanif" or "Sabiens" (Rational Believers).

The concept that God is one implies two significant issues about humankind; first, all humans are equal, simply because we are descendants of Adam and Eve. All of the humankind is a family—brothers and sisters, equal before God, differentiated only by the nobility of actions, not by color or gender. Showing preference for one human over another by accidents of birth, like gender, color, or ethnicity is unjust and violates reason and ethics. Second, we have certain inalienable liberties because we have free will granted by our Creator. The most significant choice is to accept or reject God, our Creator. Every other choice is second to this, including the freedom to choose between a host of right and wrong actions to the freedom to choose our spouse, friends or profession rather than being born into them. (16)

Today Muslims, Christians, and Jews regard Abraham as their patriarch. He founded a sustained monotheistic society subscribing to the belief that there is only one God, the Creator, and Sustainer of the Universe. Their Prophets are direct descendants from Abraham's sons, Muhammad from the elder, Ishmael, and Moses, David and Jesus from Isaac. The message of Quran is to reform the moral and social systems as per Abraham's monotheism: *"Say: Surely, my Lord has guided me to the right path; the right religion, the faith of Abraham the upstanding, and he was not of the polytheists"* (Quran 6:61).

The Quran emphasizes the universality of Abraham's faith, refers to Abraham as the leader of humankind (Quran 2:124), and tells Muslims that the faith of your father Abraham is your faith (Quran 22:78). The Quran commands Muslims to follow Abraham's faith: *"And who is better in faith than the one who submits his face to God and is good in deeds and follows the creed of Abraham, the upstanding. God made Abraham a friend"* (Quran 4:125).

The Bible teaches that those who lived without knowing Moses or Jesus and have faith in God will be saved. God will examine their faith in Him. (17) "And Abram believed the Lord, and the Lord counted him as righteous because of his faith" (Genesis15:6). Abraham has been the key person, servant of God and model of reason-based faith and unity of believers.

People of the Bible

Jews and Christians are referred in the Quran as "People of the Bible" About two-thirds of the Quran chapters allude to the Bible and mention Adam, Abraham, Moses, David, Solomon, and Jesus. Moses leading children of Israel out of bondage is the most mentioned prophet in the Quran. The Quran recounts the story of David slaying Goliath and describes David as a singer of God's praises Psalms: *"O David, We have made you a vicegerent, so judge between people with the truth"* (Quran 38:26). An entire chapter of the Quran, Mary, deals with her and Jesus. Jesus and Mary are also mentioned in many other verses.

Jews and Christians are viewed as fellow believers in the One God and the recipients of scriptures from Him. Muslims believe in the Biblical prophets as Islamic prophets. The three religions share a common moral code, *"Say: We believe in God, and the revelation given to us, and the revelations given to Abraham, Ishmael, Isaac, Jacob and the Tribes, and that given to Moses and Jesus, and that given to (all) the prophets from their Lord: We make no distinction among them, and to Him we are submitters"* (Quran 2:136).

Muslims are permitted to eat the food offered by the Jews and Christians unless specifically prohibited, such as alcohol or pork. They reciprocate by offering their food to them: *"The food of the People of the Book is lawful unto you, and your food is lawful unto them"* (Quran 5:5). Further, a Muslim man is permitted to marry (the most intimate relation and sacred bond) a Jewish or Christian woman.

Judaism, Christianity, and Islam are variations of the same basic religion. All believe in one God, Creator of the universe. All have a similar line of prophets. All recognize the traditions contained in the Book of Genesis. Many stories of the Bible are mentioned in the Quran. (18) All acknowledge the Ten Commandments and honor Abraham's faith. So what is the difference?

Islam in contrast to Judaism

1) In Islam, God is sovereign, perfect, transcends human challenge. The idea of "wrestling with God" is replaced with submitting to God.

2) Islam highlights notions of Judgment Day and the afterlife with the focus on both faith and deeds; Faith as the motive for deeds and deeds as the translation of faith.

3) Islam honors Jesus as the true Messiah prophesied in the Hebrew Bible. Mary is chaste and virgin. Jesus was the messenger of God to children of Israel. God blessed Mary and Jesus.

4) Islam has no notion of chosen people or sacred blood. Being one of God's people is something achieved individually through faith and righteous deeds. God's message is not only to the Jewish people, but it is for all humankind.

5) God's prophets are role models of faith. So they make honest mistakes but not major sins: Noah did not drink, Lot did not commit incest, Ishmael did not molest, Jacob did not steal, and David did not commit adultery, and so on.

Islam in contrast to Christianity

1) There is no notion of inherited original sin in Islam: Adam and Eve's disobedience is forgiven. Humans are born innocent; there is no baptism. Islam emphasizes both correct behavior and belief and focuses on moral law.

2) Disobedience of Adam and Eve leaves no chasm between God and humankind. Islam denies the notion that Jesus had to be crucified so that God forgives humans. God is All-Merciful and All-Powerful.

3) Salvation or repentance from sin cannot be achieved through confession to a priest or sacrifice on another's behalf. Everyone is responsible and accountable for his acts only. Forgiveness is in the domain of God alone.

4) There is no divine incarnation. God, the creator of time, space, energy and matter, is beyond them. Jesus was only a prophet and a human being, not divine. Jesus was not crucified or killed. God saved him and raised him to the heavens.

5) There is no priesthood (intermediary between a human being and God) in Islam. The Imam is no more than a knowledgeable prayer leader and brother in faith. All people are equal before God. There is no religious authority, ministry, or God's spokesman.

A Common Term

Despite the differences between Islam, Judaism, and Christianity, the Quran counsels forbearance and forgiveness to the people of the Bible (Quran 2:109). It instructs believers to argue with them nicely stating the fact that they all worship one God: *"And do not argue with the followers of the Bible except by what is best, except those of them who act unjustly, and say: We believe in what is sent to us and sent to you, and our God and your God is One, and to Him we submit"* (Quran 29:46).

The Quran reminds Muslims that some of the people of the Bible are upstanding who recite God's message throughout the night and prostrate themselves before God. They believe in God and the Last Day. They enjoin doing what is right and forbid doing what is wrong and vie with one another in doing God's work and these are among the righteous (Quran 3:113).

Both the Jews and Christians are called to a common term, Abraham's faith and interfaith dialogue: *"Say, O people of the Bible, Let us come to a common term among us. Let us worship no one except God, nor set up any rivals before Him, nor regard any of us as lords before God. However, if they turn away, tell them, bear witness that we are submitted to God"* (Quran 3:64). *"And they say: Become Jews or Christians, you will be on the right course. Say: Instead, (we follow) the faith of Abraham, the upstanding, and he was not one of the idolaters"* (Quran 2:135). (18)

Prophet Abraham did not limit faith and righteousness to one ethnic group. He did not worship a human being or pray to statues. He believed in One All-powerful God and rejected idols. He stood out for justice and called people to the truth: *"Abraham was neither a Jew nor Christian, but he was truthful in faith, submitter to God and was not one of the idolaters"* (Quran 3:67).

Who is Jesus?

According to Islam, Jesus was the true Messiah prophesied in the Hebrew Bible, a Prophet of God. He was not divine. He belonged to a long line of prophets who called their peoples throughout history to the worship of One God. These include Abraham, Moses, David, and Solomon. The Quran affirms that Jesus' birth was miraculous as that of Adam. God created Adam without father or mother and created Eve from Adam: *"Verily, the likeness of Jesus before God is similar to Adam. He created him from dust, then (He) said to him, 'be!' and he comes to be"* (Quran 3:59). The Book of Genesis illustrates the creation of light in a similar way: And God said, "Let there be light," and there was light.

Jesus is portrayed in the Quran is a prophet and messenger of God: *"(Jesus) said, I am indeed a servant of God. He has given me revelation and made me a prophet; He has made me blessed where so ever I am. He has enjoined on me prayer and charity as long as I live. He has made me kind to my mother, and not overbearing or miserable. So peace is upon me the day I was born, the day that I die, and the day that I shall be raised up to life. Such was Jesus, the son of Mary. It is a statement of truth, about which they (vainly) dispute. It is not befitting to (the majesty of) God that He should beget a son. Glory Be to Him! When He determines a matter, He only says to it, Be, and it comes to be!"* (Quran 19:30-35).

Like the accounts in the Gospels of Matthew and Luke, the Quran shows that Jesus' birth was miraculous: *"Behold! The angels said, "O Mary! God gives you glad tidings of a word from Him. His name will be Christ Jesus, the son of Mary, held in honor in this world and the Hereafter, and with those who are near to God. He shall speak to the people in childhood and maturity. He shall be of the righteous... God will teach him the book and wisdom, the Torah and the Gospel"* (Quran 3:45-48).

Not only did Jesus have a miraculous birth, but the Quran also tells us that he was born of a virgin mother and that he spoke in the cradle. Jesus performed miracles as evidence that he is the true Messiah: *"I have come to you with a sign from your Lord: I make for you out of clay, as it were, the figure of a bird, and breathe into it, and it becomes a bird by God's leave. I heal the blind, and the lepers, and I raise the dead by God's permission…"* (Quran 3:49).

Being able to perform miracles, didn't make Jesus equal to God. Everything he did was by God's permission, to teach the children of Israel about God Himself. The miracles include the Last Supper that the disciples asked him to pray to God (Quran 5:114). Even these miracles, were not enough to convince them that he was a messenger of God. The religious and political leaders tried to crucify Jesus because they were upset with his message of truth. However, God saved Jesus and raised him to Heavens. Jesus was not killed or crucified. (Quran 4:157)

In fact, the Quran is quite clear about this: *"Jesus, the son of Mary, was no more than a messenger; many were the messengers that passed away before him. His mother was a woman of truth. They had both to eat their (daily) food and walk in markets. See how God makes His signs clear to them; yet see in what ways they have deluded away from the truth!"* (Quran 5:75). Jesus himself in his words never claimed to be a god or part of Trinity. He never asked his followers to worship him.

Both Jesus and his mother had to eat food, drink water and breathe air. They were human beings, like you and me. Jesus was given the loftiest of tasks to deliver God's message to the world. However, he remained just that: a man who ate food. Some of the early followers of Jesus, out of exaggerated love viewed him more than a prophet, a god. The writings of Saint Paul influenced them. They confused the beautiful message he brought with the One who sent it. They saw the gift of Jesus to calm the winds and the seas, or cure the sick, as indicating that he was more than just a prophet.

The Quran tells us what God will say to Jesus on the Day of Judgment when He Almighty calls all people to Himself: *"And behold! God will say (on the Day of Judgment): 'O Jesus, the son of Mary! Did you say unto humankind, worship me and my mother as gods in derogation of God?' He will say: 'Glory to You! Never could I say what I had no right (to say). Had I said such a thing, You would indeed have known it. You know what is in my heart, though I know not what is in Yours. For You know in full all that is hidden. Never did I say to them anything except what You commanded me to say: "Worship God, my Lord, and your Lord." And I was a witness over them while I lived among them. When You took me up, You were the Watcher over them, and You are a Witness to all things.'"* (Quran 5:116-7).

Some biblical scholars and free thinkers have reasoned similar conclusions to Islam about refuting the divinity of Jesus and the authenticity of the Bible. *New York Times* bestselling author and Bible expert Bart Ehrman concludes that the concept of Jesus as a divine is not what the original disciples believed during Jesus's lifetime and it is not what Jesus claimed about himself. (19) (20) As a scholar, he contends that various early scribes altered the New Testament texts over the years. (21) (22)

As per the Bible, the true Messiah shall not be crucified. Crucifixion makes Jesus accursed by the pronouncement. (23) (Deut. 21:23) Jesus did not preach salvation through the atonement. Killing an innocent human being is a crime, not a way of atonement or salvation. The term Trinity is not found anywhere in the Bible. The concept of someone atoning for the sins of others is rejected in the Old Testament. (Deut.24:16, Ezekiel 18:2) The Hebrew Bible teaches that it is heretical for any human to claim to be God, part of God, or the literal son of God. It portrays the Messiah as a human leader (king) of the Jewish people.

Dan Brown reasoned in his novel "The Da Vinci Code" the world best seller in 2004 that Jesus was a mortal prophet, great and powerful man, but a man nonetheless. Jesus is not the son of God. The church doctrines are based on paganism. The divinity of Jesus is analogous to that of Horus (ancient Egyptian god) and Hercules (Greek divine hero, son of Zeus). The Cross icon was derived from the Egyptian Ankh. He concluded that the Bible has evolved through countless translations, additions, and revisions and that there is no definitive version of the book. (24)

Dr. Timothy Johnson, the renowned medical journalist, did not accept the idea that Jesus had to be crucified to appease God's demand for justice or payment for the sins of humankind. (25) The concept of God killing God or God is killed by his creations is illogical. Dolly (a domestic sheep) was the first mammal to be cloned from a female sheep in 1996. She was born without a father beyond sexual reproduction. As a biological analogy, Jesus, being born without a father from a virgin mother does not make him divine.

Interfaith Commandments

The messages from the Bible coincide closely with certain verses in the Quran. This is generally the case with the Ten Commandments, which are the fundamental obligations of man to God and to his fellow creations.

1) You shall have no other gods before Me: *"...There is no deity, but God"* (Quran 47:19) and "...You shall not set up rivals before God" (Quran 2:22).

2) You shall not make for yourself an idol: *"My Lord, make this a peaceful land, and protect me and my children from worshiping idols"* (Quran 14:35).

3) You shall not make wrongful use of the name of your God: *"And make not God's (name) an excuse in your oaths against doing good, or acting rightly, or making peace between persons; for God is One Who hears and knows all things"* (Quran 2:224).

4) Remember the Sabbath and keep it holy: the Sabbath was decreed for the Jews as a test (Quran 16:124). Believers are commanded to make every effort to attend the Friday noon prayer. They are permitted to go about their affairs during the rest of the day: *"O you who believe, when the Congregational Prayer is announced on Friday, you*

shall hasten to the commemoration of God, and drop all business" (Quran 62:9).

5) Honor your father and mother: *"...and your parents shall be honored. As long as one or both of them live, you shall never insult them, nor shall you shout at them; you shall treat them amiably"* (Quran 17:23).

6) You shall not murder: *"...if anyone murders any person, who had not committed murder or horrendous crimes, it shall be as if he murdered all the people"* (Quran 5:32).

7) You shall not commit adultery: *"…Do not even go close to adultery; it is a gross sin, and evil behavior"* (Quran 17:32).

8) You shall not steal: *"…They shall not steal" (Quran 60: 12) and "You shall not take each other's property by false means"* (Quran 4:29).

9) You shall not bear false witness: *"… And avoid saying falsehood"* (Quran 22:30) and *"…those (Servants of God) shall not bear false witness"* (Quran 25:72).

10) You shall not covet anything that belongs to your neighbor: *"…And do not covet what we bestowed upon any other people. Such are temporary ornaments of this life, whereby we put them to the test. What your*

Lord provides for you is far better and everlasting" (Quran 20:131).

A free thinker who reflects on the interfaith commandments will conclude that Islam stems from the Judeo-Christian tradition. Therefore, he thinks regarding the "Judeo-Christian-Islamic tradition." (3) The Islamic values overlap with other religions, two of the greatest commandments. <u>First:</u> To love God with all our heart, mind, soul, and strength and <u>Second:</u> To love our neighbors; that is, our fellow human beings—regardless of race, religion, or cultural background—as we love ourselves.

The Quran defines righteous deeds as follows: *"Righteousness is not to turn your faces towards east or west. The truly righteous are who believes in God, and the day of judgment, the angels, the book, and the prophets; (who) give money out of loving [God] to the relatives, the orphans, the indigent individuals, the needy travelers (including refugees), to those who ask and for freeing humans from bondage. [The truly righteous] is who perform ritual prayer and charity duty. They are who honor their covenants and be steadfast and patient in adversity, hardship, and time of striving. Such are the people of truth, the pious"* (Quran 2:177).

Let us compare this quotation to Jesus' reply to a Jewish religious teacher who asked him; which of all the teachings of God was the most important? Jesus answered; this is the first commandment: *"Hear, O Israel.*

The Lord our God, the Lord, is One, and you shall love the Lord your God with all your heart, and with all your soul, and with all your mind, and with all your strength," and the second is this: *"You shall love your neighbor as yourself" There is no other commandment greater than these"* (Mark 12:28-34). Incidentally, Jesus was not the first to use these words as teaching. He was quoting what was called the Shema and the Torah commandment to love your neighbor as yourself (Leviticus 19, 18).

The Shema flows from the assertion of the oneness of God. In the first portion, there is a commandment to love God with all one's heart, soul, and might and to remember and teach these words throughout the day. The second portion says that obeying these commands will lead to rewards, and disobeying them will lead to punishment. The third portion is a practical reminder to ensure fulfillment of these key commands, wearing the fringes: "That you may remember and do all my commandments, and be holy unto your God" Numbers 15:40). (12)

What Muslims do, is fulfill the first commandment through acts of worship: the ritual prayer, fasting, and pilgrimage. All these actions express and are devoted to the primary pillar of faith: adoration and remembrance of the one God. At a social level, Muslims fulfill the second commandment through a strong sense of valuing community over individualism and teaching a deep-seated responsibility to help others and have practical compassion through charity duty, almsgiving and care of orphans and indigent individuals. (26)

In the past, Muslims successfully institutionalized the second commandment by establishing pluralistic societies that respected religious, racial, and ethnic differences while including them all within the greater community. An example is a court system that decided cases according to different religions' laws. Laws were applied based upon the litigants' beliefs, especially in matters of marriage and divorce, custody, and inheritance. Such individualized judicial systems spread over Muslim, Jewish, and Christian communities in the Middle East and Muslim, Hindu, and other religious communities in South Asia. A Christian couple engaging in a custody case, for example, could opt to have their case heard under the Christian law.

For many centuries, Islam inspired civilizations that were particularly tolerant and pluralistic. From 800 to 1200 CE, for example, the Cordoba Caliphate ruled much of today's Spain amid a rich flowering of art, culture, philosophy, and science. Many Jewish and Christian artists and intellectuals immigrated to Cordoba during this period to escape the most oppressive regimes that reigned over Europe's Dark and Middle Ages. Great Jewish philosophers such as Maimonides were free to create their historic works within the pluralistic culture of Islam. Islam is the religion of peaceful coexistence, justice, equality, compassion, and service to humanity. There is no record of crusade, inquisition, holocaust or witch-hunt in such civilizations. (16) This model promotes peace, interfaith dialogue, and collaboration for the common good.

Pillars of Worship

Muslims affirm the essence of the five pillars of worship in the Islamic faith:

1) Declaration of Faith: Witnessing that there is no deity, but God and that Muhammad is His messenger.
2) Performing the ritual prayer at its appointed times and in a prescribed manner.
3) Charity duty: Paying charity incumbent upon all who are financially capable.
4) Fasting during the month of Ramadan, if physically able.
5) Pilgrimage to Mecca once during a lifetime, if financially and physically capable.

Islam does not teach or accept mere ritualism. Islam emphasizes intention and action. Besides these pillars, every action is done with the awareness that it fulfills God's commandments and is also considered an act of worship. To worship God is to know him and love him, to act upon his law in every aspect of life, to enjoin goodness and forbid wrong doings and oppression, to practice justice and serving the community. (27)

Declaration of Faith

The first form of worship is the declaration of one's faith with a pure intention, through affirmation that there is no deity but God and that Muhammad is the messenger and servant of God. This is the password to Islam. Observant Muslims repeat this formula on a daily basis as part of the prayer. Islam commands faith in the One God, Unique, Incomparable, and Merciful Creator and Sustainer of the Universe; faith in the Angels created by Him; faith in the Prophets through whom His revelations were brought to humankind; faith in the Day of Judgment and individual accountability for actions; faith in God's complete authority over destiny, be it good or bad; faith in life after death. (27) Muslims believe that God sent his messengers and prophets to all people and God's final message to humanity, a reconfirmation of the eternal message and a summing-up of all that had gone before, "In matters of faith, He has ordained for you what He has enjoined upon Abraham, Moses, and Jesus" (Quran 43:13).

Ritual Prayer

The second pillar of worship is the ritual prayer, a combination of praise of God and recitation of the Quran. The Prayer is the cornerstone of daily Islamic spiritual discipline. All Muslim who have reached the age of maturity and discretion are required to perform Prayer. Personal prayer (supplication to God for help, forgiveness, and guidance) is a part of ritual prayer.

Prayer is performed five times a day, during specified times, dawn, noon, afternoon, sunset and night. The start of each prayer time may be announced by the call to prayer. (27)

Before prayer, one must be in a state of physical cleanliness and ritual purity. Ritual purity is achieved by performing Ablution, a rinsing of hands, forearms, face and feet with water. Ablution symbolizes washing away of sins. Ritual purity is broken when bodily fluids (blood, excreta, and genital fluids) exit the body. The Muslim has to wash all his or her body (shower) after sex before being able to perform ritual prayer: *"God loves those who turn to him in repentance and purify themselves"* (Quran 2:222).

Performing a prayer begins with standing at attention, with one's face in the direction of the "Ka'ba" located in Mecca (Qibla). Next, one makes a formal intention of worship. The prayer begins with the praise "Allahu Akbar" which means that God is indefinitely greater than anything or everything. This also marks the start of the first prayer cycle (Rak'a). Every prayer cycle includes a recitation of the first chapter of the Quran, called the opening:

> *"Praise is due to God, Lord of the universe, the Compassionate, the Merciful, Sovereign of the day of Judgment. You alone, we worship, and to You alone, we turn for help. Guide us to the straight*

path; the path of those whom You have favored, not of those who have incurred wrath, nor of those who have gone astray". Amen

The number of cycles in each Prayer is dawn (2), noon (4), afternoon (4), sunset (3) and night (4). While each prayer cycle differs slightly, the basic structure is as follows: 1. Recitation of the opening chapter in all cycles and additional some verses of Quran, all in standing position. 2. Words of praise said in a bowing position "Glory be to my Lord, the Great." This is followed by standing saying, "God listens to those who praise Him." "Our Lord, praise is due to You only." 3. Words of praise said in a position of prostration "Glory be to my Lord, the Exalted." This is followed by sitting and double prostration after praying, "O our Lord, forgive us and have Mercy on us." 4. Exaltation of God in the final sitting position: This includes greetings of peace and calling God's blessings on Muhammad, Abraham, their families, and all righteous servants of God, and the testimony of faith, I bear witness that no deity but God, Muhamad is His servant and messenger.

The noon prayer is held congregationally on Fridays in the mosque. This worship service begins with a sermon. All such congregational prayers, which include the Prayer of "Eid Al-Fitr" and "Eid Al-Adha", are led by an Imam (prayer leader). The Call to Prayer (Adhan) is recited as follows: "God is indefinitely grater," four times. "I declare that there's no deity but God," twice. "I declare that there's no deity but God," twice. "I declare that Muhammad is the messenger of God," twice. "Come for the Prayer," twice. "Come for Success," twice. "God is indefinitely greater" twice. "There is no deity but God." For the pre-dawn Adhan, another line is added and announced twice: "Prayer is better than sleep."

Observant Muslims think about Prayer, not as a chore but a break and a time of spiritual meditation and a link to the Creator. Prayer allows them to set aside the demands of the world and simply focus their hearts on God. Prayers give comfort in the time of loneliness and sorrow. The Quran teaches prayers to God for guidance in the time of decision, protection in the time of danger, courage in the time of fear, peace in the time of turmoil, rest in the time of weariness and strength in the time of temptation. Examples of such prayers include:

> *"Our Lord: provide us with mercy from Your Own and with guidance in our matters"* (Quran 18:10). *"Our Lord: forgive me, my parents and the believers in the Day of Judgment"* (Quran 14:41). *"Our Lord: let not our hearts deviate after you have guided us and grant us mercy from Your Own"* (Quran 3:8). *"Our Lord: bestow patience upon us and take our souls submitting to you"* (Quran 7:126). *"O my Lord: enlighten my heart and ease*

my task for me and make my tongue loose so that my speech is understood" (Quran 20:25-26). *"My Lord, grant me wisdom and include me with the righteous"* (Quran 26:83).

Prayers can be offered anywhere, a place that is clean. That is why you see Muslims praying in offices, factories, schools, bus stations, airports, hospitals or farm fields. Muslims pray when it is time to pray, regardless of where they are. All they need to do is to figure out the direction of Mecca, turn toward it and begin the worship. Travelers have the choice of performing two prayers together or a shortened prayer, usually half: *"When you go forth in the land, it is permissible for you to shorten the prayer"* (Quran 4:101).

Charity Duty

One of the most important principles of Islam is that all things belong to God and that wealth is therefore held by human beings in trust. Charity (Zakat) is the third pillar of worship. The word Zakat means both purification and growth. Our possessions are purified by setting aside a proportion for those in need, and, like the pruning of plants, this cutting back balances and encourages new growth. Zakat does not only purify the property of the contributor but also purifies his heart from selfishness and greed. It also purifies the heart of the recipient from envy, jealousy, hatred, and uneasiness.

Charity duty fosters good-will and warm wishes for the contributors. (27)

In general, what remains over and above the meeting of needs and expenses, and is hoarded for the full span of one year, is liable to Zakat. The Zakat is calculated as 2.5 percent of annual savings that are above the charity threshold (90.8 grams gold or 594 g silver). It is estimated to be 5% on agriculture being taken care of by a farmer who is planting and irrigating by a machine. It is 10% of a farmer's product if it is being irrigated by rain. 20% of resources like oil or precious metals (i.e. gold, silver) are due to charity.

Zakat or charity duty is the right of the poor in the wealth of the rich and is not discretional or just philanthropy. The Quran describes eight categories of people who are to receive Zakat as follows: the poor, needy, collection workers, sympathizers, and slaves, those with debt burden, traveling aliens (including refugees) and for serving the cause of God. Charity duty is worship as means of spiritual purification and economic growth. It serves the socio-financial system by re-distributing the wealth among the community. As Muslims pay the Zakat, they have the genuine feeling that it is an investment and not a debit helping to establish economic balance and social justice.

Fasting Ramadan

Ramadan is the ninth month of the Islamic lunar calendar. All physically mature and healthy Muslims are obliged to fast from dawn to sunset daily for the complete month. They abstain from all food, drink, and any sexual contact. The sick and those who are traveling may defer their fast until their illness or journey is over. Those who cannot fast shall feed a needy person for every missed day if they can afford it. Fasting is done as an act of worship and obedience to God. It is a time to exercise critical thinking about the purpose of life and have self-control and spiritual enlightenment. (28)

Fasting is known to enhance self-discipline, patience, gratitude, sympathy, honesty, conscience and spiritual struggle. Muslims focus on worshiping God through prayer, charity, kindness, sharing and pursuing good deeds as per the Quran's commandments. Muslim children are not required to fast until they reach the age of puberty. However, in many families, younger children enjoy participating and are encouraged to practice their fasting. It is common for a younger child to fast for part of a day, or for one day on the weekend. They may collect money to donate to the needy; help prepare meals for breaking the day's fast, join congregational prayers and read Quran with the family.

Feeding Charity (Zakat Al-Fitr) is for Muslims to give food or money on behalf of fasting people. The food or money is equal to one day's meals for one person. The head of the family pays this amount for each member. *"And they feed, for the love of God, the indigent, the orphan, and the captive. (Saying) We feed you for the sake of God: no reward do we desire from you, nor thanks"* (Quran 76:8-9). Festival of Breaking the Fast (Eid Al-Fitr) marks the end of the fasting period. Muslims prepare foods and buy gifts for their family and friends and for giving to the poor and needy in the community. Congregational prayers are held in the early morning and followed by a feast and visiting relatives and friends.

Hajj (Pilgrimage)

The fifth pillar of worship is the pilgrimage, or Hajj, to the city of Mecca. Performing the Hajj once during one's lifetime is an obligation for every Muslim who is financially and physically capable of doing so. The Hajj commemorates the story of Abraham and his family and exemplifies human brotherhood of all nations and races. Each ritual step of the Hajj is completed in a spirit of introspection, penitence, thanksgiving and praise to God. (29)

Over two million people go to Mecca each year from every corner of the globe providing a unique opportunity for those of different nations to meet one another. The annual Hajj begins in the twelfth month of the Islamic lunar year. Pilgrims wear special clothes: simple garments that strip away distinctions of class and culture. They all stand equal before God. The rites of the Hajj originate from the time of the Prophet and Patriarch, Abraham.

The Hajj rite starts with entering ritual purity state called Ihram. After ritual physical cleaning, the male pilgrims wear simple white garments while female pilgrims wear modest white clothing. Ihram is a state of sanctity: celibacy and nonviolence, no hunting and no arguments. The pilgrims chant *"Here I am, O Lord, Here I am at service, You have no partner, Here I am."* The pilgrims enter the great mosque and circle the Ka'ba seven times counterclockwise. Afterward, they jog seven times between the hills of Safa and Marwa as did Hagar (Abraham's wife) during her search for water until it sprang from the well. Without this well, Mecca could not ever exist. The pilgrims drink from that well and remember God's compassion to those who are in need.

The pilgrims later stand together in the plains of Arafat (a large expanse of desert outside Mecca) and join in prayer and supplication for God's forgiveness. Staying at Arafat for the day until sunset is the centerpiece of the Hajj. It is often thought as a preview of the Day of Judgment. Here, Prophet Muhammad gave his last sermon and warned humankind. *"You will meet your Lord, and you will be accountable for your actions."*

The pilgrims pelt pebbles at three pillars that mark the three spots where Abraham, Hagar, and Ishmael stoned Satan for tempting them. Pelting pebbles are symbolic for fighting the temptation of Satan. This rite resembles Jesus refusing temptations of Satan. Afterward, the pilgrims sacrifice a sheep, goat or a camel. Keeping symbolic portion for themselves, they donate most of the meat, which is frozen, packaged and shipped to the poor worldwide.

The Hajj is not over after the end of Ihram. The pilgrims must stay in Mina two more nights in meditation on the open ground, going back to the basics of life. Observant Muslims experience Hajj as the true equality of humankind. All human colors and social levels stand together to worship one God, Creator of the Universe. Additionally, Pilgrimage has been the annual Islamic convention. People from all over the world get to know each other, learn from each other and exchange ideas and products. (30)

Muslims worldwide honor Abraham's faith by a festival (Eid Al Adha). They celebrate with prayers and the exchange of gifts in Muslim communities everywhere. On the Sacrifice Feast, Muslims sacrifice a domestic animal -- a sheep, goat, cow, buffalo or camel -- as a symbol of Abraham's sacrifice, and divide the meat among the family members, friends, relatives, and the poor. This and Eid Al Fitr, a festive day celebrating the end of Ramadan, are the two major holidays of the Islamic calendar.

Code of Ethics

The goal of Islamic lifestyle is the welfare of the people, in this world and in the hereafter which is the preservation and protection of (1) life, (2) mind, (3) religion, (4) property, and (5) procreation with the principle "No harm nor reciprocating Harm." Charity, honesty, compassion, self-control, and integrity are the goals of a Muslim, while dishonesty, violent behavior, greed, jealousy, and gossip are sins. Believers are commanded in many verses of the Quran to do justice, love kindness, walk humbly, do good to your neighbors and honor the Ten Commandments (Quran: 4:36). Common ethics of Islam include:

1. **Sanctity of human life:** Believers are commanded not to engage in mercy killings fearing starvation and not commit suicide: *"Kill not your children for fear of being destitute; We shall provide sustenance for them as well as for you. Verily the killing of them is a great sin"* (Quran 17:31) and *"And do not kill yourselves; God is merciful to you"* (Quran 4:29).

2. **Care for orphans and widows:** *"Come not near to the orphan's property except to improve it, until he attains the age of full strength..."* (Quran 17:34).

3. **Keep promises and honor contracts:** *"O you who believe, Fulfill your contracts"* (Quran 5:1) and *"(Successful indeed are the believers)...who are keepers of their trusts and their covenant..."* (Quran 23:8).

4. **Be honest and fair in transactions:** *"Give full measure, when you measure and weigh with an even balance; that is the fairest and best procedure"* (Quran 17:35).

5. **Have intellectual integrity:** *"And pursue not that of which you have no knowledge; for every act of hearing, or of seeing or of (feeling in) the heart will be enquired [on the Day of Judgment]"* (Quran 17:36).

6. **No arrogance or racism:** *"Nor walk on the earth with insolence: for you cannot crack the earth, nor stretch as the mountains in height"* (Quran 17:37) and *"God does not like anyone who is arrogant or over proud"* (Quran 31:18).

7. **Be steadfast in battles:** Believers are commanded to be steadfast during defending their religion and not to surrender during the active fight (Quran 8:15). Any person who dies or is killed in the path of God shall go to the paradise (Quran 9:111).

8. **No double standard:** The Quran forbids double standards when weighing and measuring of commodities: *"Woe to the curtailers, who, when they*

measure something to receive from people, take it in full and when they measure or weight something to give to them, give less than due" (Quran 83:1-3).

9. **No intoxicants or gambling:** *"O you who believe, intoxicants, gambling, Idols' altars and divining arrows, are uncleanness of Satan work. Therefore, refrain from it so that you may succeed. Satan wants to plant enmity and malice between you through intoxicants and Gambling and keep you off from the remembrance of God and prayer. Would you then abstain?"* (Quran 5:90-91).

10. **No cheating, fraud or bribing:** Cheating is a form of injustice, *"And do not take your properties among yourselves by false means or give it to authorities [as a bribe] so that you may take a part of the properties of other people wrongfully while you know"* (Quran 2:188).

11. **Cooperate in goodness and piety:** Islam enjoins teamwork and collaboration for the common good: *"...Help one another in goodness and piety, and do not help one another in sin and aggression..."* (Quran 5:2).

12. **Courtesy in greeting:** *"And when you are greeted with a greeting, greet with a better (greeting) than it or return it; surely God takes account of all things"* (Quran 4:86).

13. **Be mindful of God and truthful:** *"O you who believe; be mindful of God and be with the truthful"* (Quran 9-119).

14. **No slander, backbiting, or ridicule:** The Quran commands human beings to be protected from defamation, sarcasm, offensive nicknames, and backbiting. It also states that no person is to be maligned on the grounds of assumed guilt and that those who engage in malicious scandal mongering shall be punished (Quran 49: 11-12) and (Quran 24: 16-19).

15. **Consult in governance:** Prophet Muhammad, even though he was the recipient of divine revelation, was required to consult Muslims in public affairs: *"...and consult with them upon the conduct of affairs. And...When you are resolved, then put your trust in God"* (Quran 3:159). Therefore, the concept of mutual consultation "Shura" is mandatory, *"And their business is conducted through consulting each other"* (Quran 42:38).

16. **No hypocrisy or deception:** Believers are commanded to be sincere and straightforward: *"O you who believe why you say what you do not do? It is very hateful in God's perspectives to say what you do not do"* (Quran: 61: 2-3).

17. **The Virtue of work:** Work ethics are highly valued in the Quran, *"And say work, God will see your work, and (so will) His messenger and the believers"* (Quran 9:105).

18. **Keep healthy, No overindulgence:** *"O Children of Adam! Take your adorning apparel, at every prayer site and eat and drink but overindulge not. God does not like those who overindulge"* (Quran 7:31).

19. **Be not miserly or wasteful:** Islam teaches moderation in spending and utilization of resources, *"Thus you shall not keep your hand yoked to your neck out of stinginess, nor extend it to the utmost extent in extravagance"* (Quran 17:29) and *"...But squander not [your wealth] in the manner of a spendthrift [wastefulness]. Verily, spendthrifts are brothers of the Satan..."* (Quran 17:26-27).

20. **Have an assertive attitude:** Believers are commanded to have a positive attitude not be aggressive or passive, *"Be righteous as commanded and those who repent with you. And incline not toward those who do wrong and transgress not; He is All-Seer of what you do"* (Quran 11-112-3).

21. **Keep hope alive:** Hope and faith are crucial for thriving and leading a purposeful life, *"Say nothing can happen to us except what God has ordained for us. He is our Guardian. In God, believers shall*

trust" (Quran 9: 51) and *"So lose not heart or despair not…" (Quran 3:139).*

22. **Develop Goodness:** Islam commands believers to reflect and improve character. Performing prayer and other acts of worship inspires believers to develop goodness and forbids evil (Quran 29:45)

23. **Be patient and tolerant:** The Quran commands believers to be steadfast and tolerate hardships. *"O you who believe; be patient, enduring and ready and revere God so that you may succeed"* (Quran 3:200).

24. **Keep records and documents:** Muslims are commanded to keep the record of debts and key business documents. All contracts should be witnessed by two persons (Quran 2:282).

25. **Eat lawful food:** It is unlawful for Muslims to eat pork products, blood or dead animals (Quran 16:115). Animals have to be slaughtered with the memorization, *"God is the Greatest"*. Seafood and sea hunts are lawful (Halal) to eat.

Mercy and Forgiveness

The Quran highlights that God mandated mercy on Himself and is willing to forgive if a person repents (Quran 6:12). The themes of mercy and forgiveness run through many passages related to God, His Prophet, and the believers (Quran 24:22). God wants humans to be merciful to self and all of His creations. Forgiveness in Islam is not granted because of bloodline or faith in the crucifixion of Jesus for atonement. Forgiveness is open to the pious and those who do good deeds. True believers have to be assertive and repent.

Islam teaches that when someone commits a sin, it will be held against him or her on Judgment Day. To repent, The Muslim has to feel remorseful about the sin, pray: *"My Lord, forgive me"* make restitution if applicable and resolve never to redo. God has promised to forgive our sins if we seek His forgiveness sincerely. Sins are not inherited or transferred. The sinner cannot blame others or genetics for his acts. They cannot rationalize dishonesty with excuses or sins as the will of God. (28)

Forgiveness and Paradise are portrayed in the Quran as follows: *"Vie with one another towards forgiveness from your Lord and towards a paradise; the width of which spans the heavens and the earth. It has been prepared for the God Conscious, the ones who spend (for God's sake) in prosperity and adversity, and those who control anger and forgive people. And God loves those who are good in their deeds, and those who, when they happen to commit a shameful act or wrong themselves, remember God, then, seek forgiveness for their sins and who is there to forgive sins except God? And do not persist in what they have done, knowingly. Their reward is forgiveness from their Lord and gardens beneath which rivers flow where they shall live forever. And excellence is the reward of those who work"* (Quran 3:133-136).

No sin is too great for God's forgiveness: *"Say, O My servants who have transgressed against themselves: despair not of the mercy of God, for God forgives all sins, for He is Oft-Forgiving, Most-Merciful"* (Quran 39:53). Devoid of the concept of atonement for sin by the blood of Jesus and the concept of a chosen race, Muslims' great hope in God's forgiveness is expressed by being themselves forgivers, *"And let them forgive, and let them forgo: don't you love that God should forgive you?"* (Quran 24:22).

An individual can ask God anytime, anyplace, for forgiveness directly; he or she needs no intermediary or intercession, for every person, male or female, has direct access to their Creator: whenever they cry for mercy and forgiveness, He responds and forgives. There is no concept of confession or burnt offering to atone for sin. Forgiveness is the domain of God alone, and no one else has the authority to grant forgiveness. There is no certificate of indulgence or religious authority in Islam. Salvation requires both faith and deeds; Faith as the motive of deeds and deeds as the proof of faith. Faith is tested and expressed in action. God gives us the free will to have faith or not as well as to act upon His commandments or not.

The role of forgiveness, whether between individuals, tribes or nations, is the essence of Islam. Even when the law intervenes by meting out a punishment commensurate with aggression, the wronged party is encouraged to forgive: *"The recompense for an injury is an injury equal to it (in degree), but if a person forgives and makes reconciliation, his reward is due from God"* (Quran 42:40).

Observant Muslims reflect on life and learn from mistakes. They figure out what went wrong and see how to prevent them in the future. Instead of feeling embarrassed or upset, they repent to God. They reflect in a balanced way and neither focusing on strengths or weaknesses as both coexist in all of us. They look into the future and remain mindful of God (Quran 59:18).

Observant Muslims do their best and put trust in God. God loves those who trust in Him. They lead purposeful lives and reason about the wonders and creations of this universe (Quran 3:191). They do not follow anyone blindly (Quran 2:170). They listen to what is said, reason and follow the best (Quran 39:17-18). They do not follow the majority to do evil as majority is not necessarily a criterion of truth (Quran 6:116). In the bible, we find a similar commandment, (Exodus 23:2).

The Quran does not accept the idea of chosen people or the conviction that only Jews or Christians could get to the paradise. All humans are equal before God, *"They have said that no one can ever go to paradise except the Jews or Christians, but this is what they hope. Ask them to prove that their claim is true"* (Quran 2: 111).

The Quran states that anyone who believes in God and the Last Day, and work righteousness, shall have been forgiven and rewarded: *"Those who believe (in the Quran) and those who follow the Jewish (scriptures) and followers of the Christ and the Sabians (followers of Abraham faith), anyone who believes in God and the Last Day, and work righteousness, shall have their reward with the Lord: on them shall be no fear, nor shall they grieve"* (Quran 2:62).

Human Rights

The central issue of freedom and equality is the concept of human dignity. In Islam, God has conferred honor and dignity on all human beings irrespective of their race, gender, age, social status and beliefs. *"We have honored the children of Adam, and provided them with rides on land and sea. We provided for them good provisions, and we gave them greater advantages than many of our creations"* (Quran 17:70). The recognition and acceptance of all humans as children of Adam affirms the biological unity of humankind and provides the basis for the development of universal relations and global ethics. (31)

Together with human dignity and honor comes the freedom to live. All individuals have the right to be respected on an equal basis before the law and to enjoy equal social treatment. Islam stresses the equality of humankind. God created all people from a common source, and the only allegiance and obedience are to God, the Almighty Creator. Islam has never condoned any form of discrimination. The only thing that sets humans apart is their righteousness: *"O people, we created you from the same male and female, and rendered you distinct peoples and tribes, that you may recognize one another. The best among you in the sight of God is the most righteous. God is Omniscient, Cognizant"*(Quran 49:13).

The Quran prescribes freedom of religion and commands believers not only to respect others but also to guarantee freedom of faith and opinion: *"There is no compulsion in religion. Truth stands out clearly from falsehood; whoever rejects evil and believes in God has grasped the strongest rope that never breaks. And God is All- Hearing and All-Knowing"*(Quran 2:256). The life, honor and property of all citizens in a Muslim society are considered sacred whether the person is a believer or not. Racism, sexism and other forms of bigotry and prejudice violate the teachings of the Quran.

Common human rights in Islam include: (1) The Right to Life, (2) The Right to Live in Dignity, (3) The Right to Property, (4) The Right to Travel, (5) The Right of Choice, (6) The Right to Work, (7) The Right to Privacy, (8) The Right to Asylum, (9) The Right to Sustenance, (10) The Right to Knowledge.

1. Right to Life: The Quran upholds the sanctity and absolute value of human life and points out that, in essence, the life of each is comparable to that of an entire community and, therefore, should be treated with the utmost care (Quran 6: 151).

2. Right to live in dignity: The Quran (49:11-12) commands: (a) Do not let one (set of) people make

fun of another set. (b) Do not defame one another. (c) Do not insult by using nicknames. (d) Do not backbite or speak ill of one another.

3. Right to Property: People have the right to own property. The owners' rights are protected (Quran 7:10). The community ensures that these rights are protected especially those of the weak and disadvantaged (Quran 4:57).

4. Right to Travel: Islam assures the right to travel and move out especially for the oppressed peoples and religious freedom: *"Whoever moves out in the path of God, He will find flourishing in the land..."* (Quran 4:100).

5. Right of Choice: The Quran commands Prophet Muhammad to communicate the message of God and not to compel anyone to believe. The right to exercise free choice in matters of faith is endorsed and guaranteed in Islam (Quran 18: 29).

6. Right to Work: Every man and woman has the right to work, whether the work consists of gainful employment or voluntary service. The fruits of labor belong to the one who has worked for them - regardless of whether it is a man or a woman *"...to men is allotted what they earn, And to women what they earn"* (Quran 4:32).

7. Right to Privacy: *"Do not spy on one another"* (Quran 49:12). *"Do not enter any houses unless you have obtained permission and greeted their occupants"* (Quran 24:27).

8. Right to Asylum: When an oppressed person seeks refuge, it is an act of righteousness to give it to him. Every human has the right to security, *"If one amongst the non-believers ask you for asylum, grant to him so that he can hear the words of God and then escort him to where he can be secure"*(Quran 9:6).

9. Right to Sustenance: Every human being has the right to a means of living and the necessities of life. Here comes the charity duty so that resources created by God to be used for the benefit of humanity in general. Quran enjoins upon its followers, *"And in their wealth, there is acknowledged right for the needy and destitute"* (Quran 51:19).

10. Right to Acquire Knowledge: *"Read in the name of your Lord who has created. He created man out of a clot. Read, for your Lord is the most Honorable who has taught by the pen. (He) taught man what he did not know"* (Quran 96:1-5). The Quran exhorts believers to pray for advancement in knowledge (Quran 20:114).

Freedom for All

Slavery had long been practiced in pre-Islamic Egyptian, Jewish, Greek, Roman, Indian and Chinese societies in different aspects. The first document of slavery is found in clay drawings 4000 B.C. Aristotle subscribed to the idea that men were born to become unequal as some will become masters due to their superior brain power and intellectual capacity while others will become slaves. Slavery was even justified by the church especially in the colonial era because of the curse of Ham that passed to Canaan (Africans). Paul commanded slaves to obey their masters as they obey God. All people who surrender in war are enslaved as per the Hebrew Bible (Leviticus 25:44-46). (32) (31)

Slavery was widely prevalent in Arabia at the advent of Islam. The Arab's economy, like the western economy in the colonial era, was based on it. Slavery is still practiced despite being illegal because of poverty and abuse of power. (33) Slavery is almost controlled through exploitation, violence, and loss of free will. Not only did the Quran command that slaves be treated in a just and humane way (Quran 4:36), but it continually urged freeing of slaves.

People became slaves because of many reasons. Examples include unpaid debts, usury, gambling, kidnapping, poor parents who sold their children into slavery, being descendants of slaves, prisoners of war and voluntary submission to be a slave to get out from the miseries of life such as famine. Islam effectively reduces these factors through the charity duty and prohibition of usury and gambling. The Quran teaches that prisoners of war are to be set free, *"either by an act of grace or against ransom"* (Quran 47:4) and (Quran9:70-71). Islam virtually abolished slavery since the major sources of slaves were prisoners of war. Prophet Muhammad condemned slave hunting and stated that enslaving a free person is a great sin. (31)

Islam provides a package of pro-active measures to eliminate slavery as well as prevent recurrence through breaking the slavery cycle to secure true emancipation. It provides root-cause abolition of slavery and practical management plan. It is a gradual but effective approach which combines several affirmative measures. (28)

1) Islamic traditions encourage the masters and the Muslim communities setting the slaves free. The act of freeing the slave is a noble deed that is highly valued by God. The slaves themselves entered into an agreement with the masters to get their freedom by paying certain amounts of money or doing

specific tasks. Both individuals and the public were encouraged to help in providing funds for freedom.

2) The Quran prohibited the sex trade of female slaves and encouraged marriage. *"And do not compel your slave girls to prostitution, when they desire to keep chaste to get the frail good of this world's life..."* (Quran 24: 33) and *"Those who cannot afford to get married shall maintain morality until God provides for them from His grace. Those among your servants who wish to be freed to marry, you shall grant them their wish, once you realize that they are honest. And give them from God's money that He has bestowed upon you"* (Quran24:33).

3) The Quran makes the act of freeing the slave a part of repentance and getting forgiveness for sins and non-conformity of the religious rituals. There are several verses in the Quran, which specifically mentioned the requirement of freeing the slave as a way of atonement for some wrongdoings [e.g. manslaughter, breaking the oath and divorce claim] (Quran: 4:92, 5:89 and 58:3). In manslaughter, the gravity of taking a life can only be balanced by giving back a life i.e. freeing a slave.

4) The Quran commands using charity money as a financial source to free the slave: *"Charities shall go to the poor, the needy, the workers who collect them, the sympathizer, to free the slaves, to those burdened by sudden expenses, in the cause of God, and to the*

travelling aliens (including refugees). Such is God's commandment. God is Omniscient, Wise" (Quran 9:60).

5) The Quran views the freeing of slaves as an act of virtue, charity, and religious penance: *"... [The truly righteous] give the money, out of love for [God] to the relatives, the orphans, the indigent individuals, the needy travelers (including refugees), to those who ask, and to free humans form bondage..."* (Quran 2:177). *"Should not (humans) get over the steep path hurdle (to Paradise)? And do you know how? It is by freeing a slave or feeding an orphan or a needy person in a famine day"* (Quran 90:10-13). No scripture ever has commanded freeing slaves as such.

Prophet Muhammad and his companions implemented these rules as laid out in the Quran by providing the living, working personal examples in his traditions. Prophet Muhammad set his slave free. He set the unbelievers prisoners of war free for ransom. The ransom for each prisoner was to teach ten children how to read and write. He helped his companion Selman, the Persian to fulfill his freedom agreement by planting trees. His companion Abu Bakr bought Bilal, the Abyssinian from his master to set him free. (31)

Justice for All

One of the key commandments of Quran to believers is the commitment to honesty and justice. The focus of justice is equality of humankind before God, humility and piety. The Quran denounces all acts of injustice: *"Surely God commands you to deliver trusts to those entitled to them and that when you judge between people you judge with justice; surely God admonishes you with what is excellent; surely God is Seeing, Hearing"* (Quran 4:58).

Justice is one of the attributes of God. God is described in the Quran as a "God of justice" who loves justice and delights in it: *"God enjoins Justice and doing good and giving to..."* (Quran 16:90). The system in the earth and the heavens is established in a just balance. The Quran commands that the code of human conduct should be based on justice likewise (Quran 55:7-8).

Justice is a central theme both in the legal sense and spiritual sense. Fundamentally it suggests a sense of what is right and an exercise of reason and free will with a practice of judgment and responsibility. The ultimate injustice is for a person or a group to be treated unfairly or abandoned as if they were nonmembers of the human race. The common good demands justice for all, the protection of the human rights of all. Justice commanded by God is tested by how the poor, widows, orphans, and disadvantaged are treated. (28)

All members of the community have mutual rights and responsibilities. The Quran has laid down this principle clearly: *"No bearer of burdens shall be made to bear the burden of another"* (Quran 6:164). Islam believes in personal responsibility. We are responsible for our acts. The consequence of our actions cannot be transferred to someone else. It is unjust to extend punishment to the family or community of the accused person.

The Quran commands that duty to balance ability and responsibility to match authority: *"We do not impose on any soul a duty except to the extent of its ability; and when you speak, then be just though it be (against) a relative, and fulfill God's covenant; this He has enjoined you with that you may be mindful"* (Quran 6:152). Believers are commanded to bring evidence for accusations and be fair witnesses. Taking an oath is required in all proceedings.

The Quran commands believers to deal justly with others and exercise honorable judgment: *"O you who believe, Be ever steadfast in your devotion to God, bearing witness to the truth in all equity; and never let any group's hostility lead you to deviate from Justice. Be Just: this is closest to being God Conscious. And be God Conscious: verily God is aware of all what you do"* (Quran 5:8-9). *"Do not let your hatred of a people incite you to aggression"* (Quran 5:2).

Deviation from Justice is not allowed even when it concerns one's parents or enemy. The ruler and the ruled, the rich and the poor, black and white should be treated equally by the law: *"O you who believe, Be ever steadfast in upholding equity, bearing witness to the truth for the sake of God, even though it be against yourselves or your parents and relatives. Whether the person concerned be rich or poor, God's claim takes precedence over either of them. Do not, then, follow your desires, lest you swerve from justice…"* (Quran 4:135).

God commands judges to rule with Justice. *"Rule with Justice and not yield to desire, lest it should turn you away from God's path"* (Quran 38:26). God is the Ultimate Judge of all humankind. The just are loved by God and will be rewarded while the unjust will be punished on the Day of Judgment, *"If they argue with you, tell them that God is knowledgeable about what you do. God will judge you on the Day of Judgment about what you dispute"* (Quran 22:68-9).

Social Justice

Social Justice and responsibility are the crucial virtues of Islamic conscience. Muslims are commanded as a first duty to build a community characterized by practical compassion. A sense of equality and collective responsibility towards one another has been the hallmark of the early Muslim community. As a result, an influx of individuals embraced Islam, to escape the brutal and rigid hierarchical social structure that prevailed in Arabia, Persia and the Roman Empire. (31)

Personal wealth is considered a trial (Quran 64:15) and a gift entrusted to the wealthy by God (Quran 57:7, 2:254, 4:39, 13:22) to see if they will handle it as He commands. The poor and the needy are therefore entitled to a share of the society's wealth (Quran 51:19, 70:24-5). Muslim civil leaders implemented the teachings of the Quran. They constructed social institutions that protect the needy and disadvantaged and ensure that they are not ignored or forgotten. No human being should be left behind. The concept that the rich get richer and the poor get poorer is not accepted. The Quran commands that the wealth of society does not circulate in the hands of a wealthy few (Quran 59:7).

Charity duty is a mandatory fixed percentage (widely accepted as 2.5%) of a Muslim's savings that the community is entitled to, every year. This worship involves material benefit to others. A charity agency collects the money and spends it specific venues listed in the Quran for the benefit of all community members, Muslims and non-Muslims alike. These venues include amongst others: the poor, the needy, the indebted, and for the liberation of slaves (Quran 2:177, 4:36, and 9:60). All gainful activities, e.g., farming, mining, industrial production and trading, have their own specific Zakat that is also due annually. The Non-Muslims pay the convention tax "Jizyah" which is equivalent to charity duty to ensure equal rights and economic equity. The convention tax is taken from the rich of non-Muslims and given to the poor.

Almsgiving is different from Charity duty in that is it not mandatory and has no preset limit. It is strongly encouraged in hundreds of verses in the Quran, as a means of obtaining God's mercy and forgiveness (Quran 24:22, 92:17-18), cleansing the souls of impurity (Quran 9:103), and attaining superior degree faith (Quran 30:38, 76:8-9, 90:10-16). Spending money on those in needs is also considered a means of expiation for different kinds of sins and mistakes (Quran 2:184, 5:89, 5:95, and 58:4). Relieving the indebted (or remitting the debt entirely) is promised a great reward by God (Quran 2:280-281).

Another kind of charity is the endowment. This is usually of larger magnitude and is in the form of an asset, e.g., a farm, factory, large building or a piece of land that should be invested with all the revenue going to charity. This choice is particularly attractive as it satisfies what is referred to as "on-going" or "everlasting" charity as per the traditions of Prophet Muhammad. This kind of charitable deed is one of only three things that Muslims believe will continue to get a reward from God after their death. The other two are knowledge and planting trees for the benefits of humans or animals: *"If any believer plants any tree, and a human being or an animal eats from it, he will be rewarded as charity."* (34)

Those who are bent on sequestering wealth, and denying the less fortunate a share in their possessions are always given as an example of the ones who will be suffering in the hereafter and are deprived of the mercy of God (Quran 3:180, 4:37, 47:38, 89:17-24). Not feeding the needy is cited amongst the major reasons for which someone will not be in paradise (Quran 74:42-46). Lack of kindness to the orphans and the needy are markings of hypocrites whose hearts are devoid of faith despite performing religious rituals (Quran 107:1-7). Amassing wealth for its sake (i.e., for the love of gathering money) is an evil deed deserving of extreme punishment on the Day of Judgment (Quran 9:35).

Muslims are instructed to spend in charity. It is interesting that the verb 'spend' is used in the Quran almost exclusively to mean spend money on someone else in need of financial help. Not only are Muslims repeatedly instructed to spend, but they are also explicitly instructed to spend from their most cherished possessions, from what is dear to them, from what they consider to be the best that they own (Quran 2:267, 3:92). Generosity in spending is a hallmark of the most dedicated believers (Quran 23:60).

Moderation in spending is commanded by the Quran. While Muslims are repeatedly encouraged to spend from their wealth in the path of God, the Quran reminds them to spend sensibly. Wastefulness is strongly admonished in the Quran and over-spending (even on charity) will cause harm that defeats the charity's purpose (Quran 17:26-29). A generous yet sensible wealthy person is, in the long term, more beneficial to the society and the poor than the unwise one that goes bankrupt (Quran 2:195).

War against Usury

The Quran strongly prohibits usury: *"Those who charge usury are in the same position as those controlled by the devil's influence. This is because they claim that usury is the same as commerce. However, God permits commerce and prohibits usury. Thus, whoever heeds this commandment from his Lord, and refrains from usury, he may keep his past earnings, and his judgment rests with God. As for those who persist in usury, they incur Hell; wherein they abide forever"* (Quran 2:275).

The Quran teaches to refrain from usury: *"God condemns usury, and blesses charities. God dislikes every disbeliever, guilty. Lo! Those who believe and do good works and establish worship and pay the poor-due, their reward is with their Lord and no fear shall come upon them neither shall they grieve. O you who believe, you shall observe God and refrain from all kinds of usury, if you are believers. If you do not, then expect a war from God and His messenger. However, if you repent, you may keep your capitals, without inflicting injustice or incurring injustice. If the debtor is unable to pay, wait for a better time. If you give up the loan as a charity, it would be better for you, if you only knew"* (Quran 2:276-280).

Believers are forbidden to charge usury. They are encouraged to give good loans and charity: *"O you who believe, you shall not take usury, compounded over and over. Observe God, that you may succeed"* (Quran 3:130), *"And for practicing usury, which was forbidden, and for consuming the people's money illicitly. We have prepared for the disbelievers among them painful retribution"* (Quran 4:161), and *"The usury that is practiced to increase some people's wealth does not gain anything with God. However, if people give to charity, seeking God's pleasure, these are the ones who receive their reward many folds"* (Quran 30:39).

Islam affirms the freedom of property owners to spend, give away, and invest. Such freedom of disposal is virtually unrestrained as long as they are not being based on cheating and swindling. Cheating infringes upon the rights of others and weakens the fabric of financial interdependence. Islam forbids the hoarding or monopolizing of goods and services, such as sources of water that are necessary for the continuation of life and that properly belong in the public domain. Such monopolies would harm the public for the sake of gain in the hands of a select few. Islam strictly forbids the giving or taking of interest on any loan in any amount. Interest is defined as a set return on loan, and as such implies a profit based on no risk or effort, a principle completely against Islamic ideals. Trade (unlike usury) is based on sharing risk, effort, and profit.

Islam encourages investment and good loans given as a means of charity. Such loans are given by Muslims with the expectation that they are paid back. However, the intention of helping a fellow human being in distress is not profit but social justice and pleasure of God. Usury has crumbled empires, enslaved many citizens and oppressed developing countries. God has promised to decrease the sustenance of the collector of usury and increase the sustenance of the one who gives alms. The almsgiving and charity duty serve as an economic stimulus package for the community that enhances redistributing wealth to shrink the gap between the rich and the poor.

Unequal societies have more poverty, more spending on the military, higher infant mortality rates, higher population percentage in prison, more homicides, greater alcohol and drug abuse, and lower life satisfaction. The economic status of the poor individuals and countries will improve if the financial institutions implement the Islamic principles of no usury, good loans and forgiving loans of the needy. For example, the heavy indebted developing countries would benefit from debt relief and no interest loan to cancel or reduce external debt repayments. This will make more funds available for food, health, and education. These Islamic principles are practical measures to break the cycle of poverty, ignorance, and disease.

Family & Community

The family is the foundation for a productive community. The peace and security offered by a stable family unit are greatly valued by Islam and considered essential for the spiritual growth of its members. Sharing and caring for each other is the foundation of Muslim families and communities. A harmonious social order is created by the existence of extended families and the establishment of mutual rights and responsibilities of father, mother, children, relatives and neighbors. (29)

Parents are greatly respected in the Islamic tradition and caring for one's elderly parents is considered an honor and a blessing. Mothers are particularly honored: the Quran teaches that since mothers endure so much during pregnancy, childbirth and child rearing, they deserve special consideration and kindness. It is stated in the Quran: *"And we have enjoined upon man to be good to his parents. With difficulty upon difficulty did his mother bear him and wean him for two years. Show gratitude to Me and your parents. To Me is the ultimate destination"* (Quran 31:14).

Marriage is greatly encouraged in Islam. It signifies the commitment of spouses to each other with love, intimacy, and respect. A Muslim marriage is both a sacred act and a legal agreement, in which either partner is free to include legitimate conditions. As a result, divorce, although uncommon, is permitted only as a last resort. The Quran presents the idea of what we today call a "no-fault" divorce and does not make adverse judgments about divorce. Marriage customs vary widely from country to country: *"And one of His signs is that He created mates for you from yourselves that you may find rest in them, and He put between you love and compassion; most surely there are signs in this for people who reflect"* (Quran 30:21).

Marriage establishes spouses' mutual rights and responsibilities and secures a nurturing environment for potential children. Children have the rights to legitimacy; loving care, and be raised by both parents. It is unfair for a single mother to take the burden of child care alone while the father does not accept responsibility or share in the care. Islam forbids sexual promiscuity and homosexuality and teaches that loyalty in a relationship is the natural, safe sex. Islam gives a sense of meaning and purpose of family life that is based on love and compassion, mutual support to cope with life events. (29)

Monogamy is the common practice among Muslims. The Bible does not ban polygamy. Prophets such as Abraham, Jacob and Solomon had more than one wife. The Quran regularized the Pre-Islamic practice of polygamy after the second war in AD 625 when 10% of the one thousand warriors were killed, leaving many widows and orphans. The Quran encouraged the believers to be fair to both groups: *"Give the orphans their property and substitute not worthless (things) for their good ones, and not devour their property; this is surely a great sin. And if you fear that you cannot act equitably towards orphans, then marry such women… two or three or four; but if you fear that you will not do justice, then marry only one…"* (Quran 4:2-3).

The teachings of Quran protect human life and property, demand respect for parents and the spouses and children of one's neighbor, and manifest a special concern for the vulnerable members of the community: widows, orphans, the poor, and aliens in the land: *"Serve God, and do not associate anything with Him, and do good to parents, kinsfolk, orphans, those in need, close neighbors, distant neighbors, the companions by your side, the traveling aliens, and the slaves: Surely, God does not like those who are arrogant and boastful"* (Quran 4:36).

Modest behavior is the key of Islamic etiquette (Quran 31:13-19). This includes being kind and respectful, thinking before acting, speaking in a quiet voice, wearing modest clothes, not staring at people, walking humbly with purpose, eating without gobbling and keeping personal hygiene and assertive attitude. Observant Muslims feel humble yet important part of the world as they do their best for peace and common good. They contribute to the welfare of their communities especially the disadvantaged.

Islam is a global faith and way of life. It is not specific to any people or region. Muslims are Egyptians, Turkish, British, French, Indians, Chinese, Americans, Africans, and Arabs by culture and citizenship. It is the Muslim's fundamental right, as well as responsibility, to participate in as many aspects of the community's life as possible and contribute to civic activities (e.g. charity). Observant Muslims in any community are honest, loyal and trustworthy because they live by the principle: *"God commands justice, the doing of good and giving to the kindred and forbids indecency, evil and offense"* (Quran 16:9).

Historically, Muslims are categorized into two sects by the tradition of who should be the Muslims leader. Sunni Muslims (majority) agree with the position taken by Prophet Muhammad's companions, that the Muslim leader should be elected from among those capable of the job. Therefore, Prophet Muhammad's close friend and advisor, Abu Bakr was elected. He became the first Caliph of the Islamic nation. The word "Sunni" in Arabic comes from a word meaning "one who follows the traditions of the Prophet. On the other hand, Shia Muslims (minority) share the belief that leadership should have stayed within the Prophet Mohammad's bloodline cousin Ali and his descendants. (28)

Later on, the Sufi groups developed after the first century. They focus on the spiritual and mystical aspects of worship. The Salafi group developed several centuries later. That group views the first three generations of Muslims as the model for worship and mannerisms. All sects accept the Quran as the divine word of God and value the traditions of the prophet Muhammed. All acknowledge the pillars of worship and interfaith commandments and so on. The differences between sects are primarily political and cultural.

The Quran calls for unity and commands not to divide into sects (Quran 30:31-32). Therefore, observant Muslims do not distinguish themselves by claiming membership in any particular group but prefer to be called simply Muslims. They implement the commandment of the Quran to follow the faith of Abraham (Quran 6:161) who called believers in God Muslims (Quran22:78). They are mindful of God's admonition never to divide in religion (Quran 6:159), and God's commandment to reconcile as believers are but one brotherhood (Quran 49:10).

Women in Islam

According to the Quran men and women are equal before God. Women are not blamed for violating the "forbidden tree" nor are their sufferings in pregnancy and childbirth a punishment for that act. Islam treats a woman, whether single or married, as an individual in her right, with the right to own and dispose of her property and earnings. A marital gift is given by the groom to the bride for her personal use, and she keeps her family name. (29)

Roles of men and women are complementary and collaborative. Rights and responsibilities of both sexes are equitable and balanced in their totality. Both men and women are expected to dress in a way that is simple, modest and dignified and keep chastity. Particular traditions of dress found in some Muslim countries are often the expression of local customs rather than religious principle. Likewise, treatment of women in some areas of the Muslim world reflects cultural practices that are inconsistent with the Quran teachings. (27)

The Quran commands kind and fair treatment of women (Quran 4:19). The Quran does not single out Eve for blame but depicts Adam and Eve as equally responsible for disobedience of God. Eve is not the temptress, nor the source of evil. She is not responsible for the fall of humanity. Islam forbids depicting God as a figurative father and does not treat fathers or fatherhood as sacred. It does not say that males embody divine attributes and that women are by nature weak. (27)

In the Quran, God often addresses both men and women, ordains similar religious duties and makes it clear that women have the same claim to paradise as men: *"Wives are garments for you while you are garments for them"* (Quran 2:187), *"The believing men and the believing women they are guardians of each other"* (Quran 9:71), *"Whoever does right, whether male or* female...We shall pay them recompense" *(Quran16:97),* "I shall not let the deeds of anyone go to waste, male or female; both are the same in this respect" (Quran 3:195), and *"Those who give alms be they men or women shall receive a rich recompense"*(Quran 57:18).

The Quran gave women marriage, divorce, and inheritance rights fourteen centuries before women in the West were granted such rights. The Quran says: *"Men shall have a share in what parents and kinsfolk leave behind, and women shall have a share in what parents and kinsfolk leave behind, whether it be little or much—a share ordained by*

God" (Quran 4:7). The females inherit half of what males do because they are not required to pay out of their wealth for the support of their dependents as males are. Women do not have to work or share with husbands family expenses.

The Quran enjoins men to be caring and kind with women, and one chapter even begins by saying: *"God has indeed heard the words of she who pleads with you concerning her husband and complains to God"* (Quran 58:1). This verse illustrates that justice between men and women—especially in the domestic context—is a matter of importance to God. Quran commands believers to stop the pre-Islam practice of female infanticide and warns all humankind about the consequences of such crime in the hereafter (Quran 81:8-9).

The Quran places equal responsibility on men and women for all religious obligations. Women are equally obliged to pray, to fast, to give charity out of their wealth, to perform the pilgrimage, and so forth. Gender equality is an intrinsic part of Islamic belief. The Quran says: *"God has prepared a forgiveness and a great reward for the submitting men and women, the believing men and women, the pious men and women, the truthful men and women, the patient men and women, the humble men and women, the charitable men and women, the fasting men and women, the men and women who guard their chastity, the men and women who remember God frequently"* (Quran 33:35).

The Muslim woman wears a scarf covering her breasts as part of modest clothing commanded by the Quran. Women are valued as human associates and not as sex objects. Modest clothing signifies this principle and gives women privacy. The scarf is similar to what a Catholic nun or an Orthodox Jewish woman wears. Virgin Mary is the model for Muslim women as far as dress is concerned. The dress code of some Muslim women reflects their local customs and cultures and not Islam. (35)

Striving for Peace

Islam permits bearing arms in self-defense, in defense of religion, or on the part of those who have been expelled forcibly from their homes. It lays down strict rules of combat that include prohibitions against harming civilians and against destroying crops, trees, and livestock. Islamic law forbids harming women, children, the elderly, noncombatants, and the environment in a wartime situation. (29) The Quran prohibits indiscriminate destruction of civilians and wildlife and warns those who contribute to this corruption Hellfire (Quran 2:204). Therefore, nuclear, chemical and biological weapons are forbidden in Islam.

Injustice would be triumphant in the world if good people were not prepared to risk their lives in a righteous cause. Peace is active through being well prepared to defend yourself, your family and your community against exploitation and aggression. One reads in the Quran: *"Fight in the cause of God against those who wage war against you but do not commit aggression. God does not like aggressors"* (Quran 2:190).

"Justice is worth fighting for," If two parties are fighting each other first all efforts must be made for an

amicable resolution. If not successful, fighting the unjustly wronged party would be necessary. If the wronged party stops, reconciliation must be done (Quran 49:9). *"If they seek peace, then you seek peace. And trust in God for He is the One that hears and knows all things"* (Quran 8:61). The Quran says: *"God forbids you not, with regards to those who fight you not for [your] faith nor drive you out of your homes, from dealing kindly and justly with them; for God loves those who are just"* (Quran, 60:8).

Therefore, war is a last resort and is subject to the rigorous conditions laid down by the sacred law. The often misunderstood and overused term jihad means "struggle or strive" and not "holy war or crusade" (a term not found anywhere in the Quran). Jihad, as an Islamic concept, can be on a personal level—inner struggle against evil within oneself; struggle for decency and goodness on the social level; and struggle on the battlefield, if and when necessary (self-defense).

The Quran explains the concept of Jihad (striving for peace in the way of God) as follows: *"… And strive in God's way as you ought to strive. He has chosen you, and has not imposed any difficulty on your way of life; it is the way of your father, Abraham. It is He (God) who named you Muslims, both before (this) and in this (the Quran), that the Messenger be a witness to you, and you be a witness to humankind. So establish the ritual prayer and give the charity duty, and hold fast to God - He is your Guardian The best Guardian and the best Helper"* (Quran 22:78).

The Quran denounces all acts of hatred and injustice and calls for peace and the initiative to do virtue: *"Virtue and evil are not equal. If you replace evil (response) by good ones, you will certainly find that your enemies will become your intimate friends. Only those who exercise patience and who have been granted a great share of God's favor can find such opportunity"* (Quran 41:34-35). The Quran acknowledges, as legitimate causes for military action, some specific situations, including defense when the community of believers is attacked and freeing oppressed people.

The Quran permits armed resistance when believers are under direct attack: *"Permission to take up arms is granted to those who are attacked; they have suffered injustice. God has all the power to give victory. Those who have been expelled from their homes without a just cause except that they say: 'Our Lord is God.' For if God had not enabled people to defend themselves against one another, monasteries, churches, synagogues and mosques, in which God's name is abundantly extolled would surely be destroyed"* (Quran 22:39-40).

The Quran commands Muslims to have "David fighting Goliath" as a role model for God's support for those who fight for a just cause and steadfast to defend themselves against tyranny (Quran 2:249-51). God grants permission to liberate weak groups that are clearly the victims of oppression: *"Why do you not fight for the cause of God or save the helpless men, women, and children who cry out, "Lord, set us free from this town of wrong doers and send us a guardian and a helper"* (Quran 4:75). However, supporting the oppressed groups shall not violate laws, contracts or treaties (Quran 8:72).

Why Do Misconceptions Exist?

Islam and Muslims are often portrayed as unreasonable, fanatical, intolerant, and violators of human rights and women's rights. These popular images come down from age-old myths and fears, often fueled by political and economic interests. Publicity is given to extremists on the margins of Muslim societies leading to prejudices and negative feelings about Islam and Muslims. These misconceptions breed suspicion, discrimination, racism and even violence. (36) Anyone who condones or commits an act of terrorism is violating the teachings of the Quran: ***"...Whoever saves a life; saves all of humankind..."*** (Quran 5:32).

Crude characterizations of Islam and Prophet Muhammad were common in Europe during the dark ages, the Christian Crusades, the Protestant, Reformation, the Inquisition and the era of European colonialism justifying slavery. Prophet Muhammad was demonized because of his last sermon and his tradition to defend the oppressed. The religious authorities viewed the Islamic principle of equality before God and the concept that no mediators between God and humankind as a threat.

Misconceptions about Islam are portrayed by the media (influence industry) in response to political and economic interests. Examples include Petroleum and its geopolitics and the assaults on reason and freedom by the use of politics of fear. (37) Some distortions are rooted because of ignorance or the presentation of half-truths and selective quotes out of contexts. (38) Some misconceptions are brought by fanatic religious leaders, who demand belief in received dogma, rather than open-ended scientific inquiry and reasoning. The fanatic's visions of the return of Jesus and the end times are emphasized with cognitive biases of self-prophecy and wishful thinking. Academic studies about Islam are ignored. Objective responses to critics are not broadcasted. (39)

The so-called radical fundamentalists are not confined to a specific religion. They could be Jews, Christians or Muslims. They represent their egos, not faith. Is American Judaism responsible for the 1994 Hebron massacre carried out by Baruch Goldstein? Is American Protestantism responsible for Timothy McVeigh who committed the 1995 Oklahoma blowing up a federal building? Is European Christianity responsible for Anders Behring Breivik, the perpetrator of the 2011 Norwegian massacre? Is Christianity responsible for the Holocaust because some Nazis used Christian doctrines to justify it? Is Christianity responsible for Apartheid in South Africa because one major church supported it? Is Christianity responsible for the Inquisition, Fascism or

Colonialization because they originated in Europe and some Christians supported them? (40)

Islam is frequently misunderstood and may seem as exotic in some parts of today's world. Perhaps this is because religion no longer dominates everyday life. The majority of average citizens know very little about Islam and 63% of Americans are completely unaware of it as per the Gallop poll January 2010. While **knowledge** is power, **ignorance** can render persons and communities vulnerable to misconceptions and errors.

The Supreme Court Judge Anthony Kennedy denounced what he called abysmal ignorance of Islam in 1998. He called on Americans to search for greater understanding of the Muslims: *"I hope that in the next century we will come to terms with our abysmal ignorance of the Muslim world. Muslims aren't a bunch of wackos and nuts. They are decent, brilliant, talented people with a great civilization and traditions of their own, including legal traditions. Americans know nothing about them. There are people in that part of the world with whom, we are simply out of touch. That's a great challenge for the next century."* (41)

Let us read the summary of Prophet Muhammad's last sermon, reflect on what he preached, and ask ourselves who is distorting the truth about Islam and why? (40)

The Last Sermon:

"There is no superiority for an Arab over a non-Arab and for a non-Arab over an Arab or for a white [person] over a black [person] or for a black [person] over a white [person], except in piety." Prophet Muhammad declared that message of equality in 632 AD. He was delivering this sermon during his only pilgrimage to Mecca. He climbed the Mount of Mercy at the valley of Arafat to deliver what amounted to his last will. He died two months later.

"Hear me, O People, for I do not know if I shall ever meet with you in this place after this year," He began, calling out "O People," and not "O Muslims," intending his words for all humankind. Emphasizing the plurality of humanity, Prophet Muhammad cited the Quran: *"O People, We created you from one male and one female, and made you into tribes and nations, so that you may know each other"* (Quran 49:13).

Speaking of the sanctity of human life and the need to end tribal savagery, Prophet Muhammad said; *"Each human's life and possessions are sacrosanct. The blood feuds of Ignorance (pre-Islamic days) are abolished. Every claim arising out of homicide is henceforth waived."* To set a personal example, Prophet Muhammad announced that he was giving up one such outstanding claim of his clan.

Prophet Muhammad declared a manifesto for economic ethic, the obligation to pay off debts and stand by financial guarantees and the duty to avoid usury and other types of exploitation: *"Your capital and your property are sacred and inviolate and yours to keep. You will neither inflict nor suffer injustice. All debts must be repaid. All borrowed property must be returned, all gifts must be reciprocated, and all financial losses compensated by the guarantors. All interest and usurious dues accruing from Ignorance (pre-Islamic days) also stand waived."* Again, leading by personal example, he said that he would pay back all the interest charged by his money-lending uncle.

Prophet Muhammad continued: *"O People, you have certain rights over your women, and your women have certain rights over you... It is for them not to commit acts of impropriety, which if they do, you are authorized to separate them from your beds and chastise them, but not harmfully... My dictum to you is that you treat women well and be kind to them; they are your partners."*

The next admonition of Prophet Muhammad, regarding the treatment of slaves, was pioneering: *"Your slaves are your brethren; See to it that you feed them with such food as you eat yourselves and clothe them with the clothes you yourselves wear. If a black slave is appointed your leader, listen to him and obey [him]."*

After reminding the believers to adhere to the teachings of the Quran, including giving charity duty and performing the Hajj, he called for solidarity of all believers: *"Believers constitute one brotherhood. Every*

Believer is a brother unto other Believers. Therefore, the property of one is unlawful to the other unless given willingly. Do not be unjust to one another." He warned against religious extremism: *"Be moderate in religious matters, for excesses caused the destruction of earlier communities."*

Prophet Muhammad concluded: *"O People, you will meet your Lord and be accountable for your actions. Have I faithfully delivered unto you my message?"* he asked. *"O God's Messenger, Yes,"* replied the multitude. The Prophet raised his forefingers and said *"O Lord, bear witness."* At sunset, he mounted his camel followed by the rest. As a commotion broke out, he called out *"Gently, gently, in the quietness of soul! And let the strong among you have a care for the weak."* (42)

Why Islam?

An observant Muslim was asked by one of his neighbors "I have known you for years; you are a very nice and smart guy. I wonder why you are a Muslim." He responded, "Why I am a Muslim? Good Question! What do you know about Islam?" His neighbor replied "Not much, but I heard from the media…" The observant Muslim listened for a while and then he said, "Please read about Islam with an open heart and mind and reason to know the truth. Here is the answer."

I am a Muslim because I am all free:

- My faith is free, as I believe in one God, Creator of the universe.
- My mind is free, as there are no intoxicants or blinding dogma.
- My heart is free, as there is no racism, hatred, or arrogance.
- My soul is free, as there is no original sin or religious authority.
- My will is free, as there is no inquisition or coercion in religion.

- My vision is free, as reasoning is the root of Islamic knowledge.
- My worship is free, as there is no mediator between God and me.
- My spirit is free, as there are sharing and justice for all humankind.
- My body is free, as there is no promiscuity or overindulgence.
- My property is free, as there is no usury, gambling, or fraud.

With freedom comes responsibility. Therefore, I am accountable for my deeds before God, Our Creator. God is the Judge of humankind. Live by reason and virtue, trust in the Lord, and do what is best. Think for yourself. These principles comprise the key message of Islam to all: "Peace be upon you."

Era of Hope

At the heart of the world's problems, lies an unsustainable economic system, based on self-interest and competition, that has failed to secure universal human rights for the majority world, and continues to inflict irrevocable harm on the environment. Soaring capital flows, a debt-based consumer culture, lobbying officials, double standards, exploitation, greed, fraud, and unfair trade, all contributed to the crisis. Poverty, unemployment, disease, illiteracy, crime, addiction, suicide, promiscuity, and violence are increasing at a fearful rate. There is practically no respect for law or religion among millions of people. On the international scene, individuals and nations live in fear and stress because they know that the so-called treaties of peace or international laws are not honored. The question now is how to solve the problems and mitigate the crisis. Therefore, the code of ethics in the Quran comes as the hope for all humankind to get freedom, justice, and moral reform.

Islam Quick Quiz

Mark T for true, F for false for each statement.

Leave it blank, if you do not know.

1) Whom do Muslims worship?
   a) Allah, the Arabic word for God ____
   b) Allah, the Creator of the universe ____
   c) Allah, the God of Abraham ____
   d) Same God of the Bible ____
   e) Prophet Muhammad ____

2) Who are the Prophets of Islam?
   a) Abraham ____
   b) Moses ____
   c) Muhammad ____
   d) Jesus ____
   e) Buddha ____

3) Who are Muslims and where do they live?
   a) Muslims constitute about 20% world population ____
   b) Only 20% of Muslims are Arabs ____
   c) All Arabs are Muslims ____
   d) Most Muslims are Arabs ____
   e) The largest Muslim population lives in Indonesia ____

4) What are the Commandments of Islam?
    a) You shall have no deity before God ____
    b) You shall not murder ____
    c) You shall not commit Adultery ____
    d) You shall not steal ____
    e) You shall not bear false witness____

5) What are the Human rights in Islam?
    a) All humans are equal before God ____
    b) No Coercion in religion ____
    c) No harm or reciprocating harm ____
    d) Quran persuades believers to free slaves ____
    e) Quran commands believers to be Just ____

6) What are the Women rights in Islam?
    a) Women and men are equal before God ____
    b) The right to work and own property ____
    c) Men and women have complementary roles ____
    d) The right to marry and initiate divorce ____
    e) Eve is responsible for the original sin ____

7) What is the meaning of Jihad in Islam?
    a) Self-defense war when necessary ____
    b) Holy war against non-Muslims ____
    c) Striving for personal improvement ____
    d) Struggling to do good deeds ____
    e) Inner struggle against evil ____

8) How is Social Justice assured in Islam?
   a) No usury ____
   b) No gambling ____
   c) No monopoly ____
   d) Sharing of resources ____
   e) Charity duty ____

9) What are the Pillars of Islam?
   a) Ritual prayer ____
   b) Fasting Ramadan ____
   c) Pilgrimage to Mecca ____
   d) Charity duty ____
   e) Communion service ____

10) How is Salvation obtained in Islam?
   a. Sincere Repentance ____
   b. Sacred Bloodline ____
   c. Crucifixion of Jesus ____
   d. Faith and Deeds ____
   e. Confession to a priest ____

Answers Key

1) A-T, B-T, C-T, D-T, E-F
2) A-T, B-T, C-T, D-T, E-F
3) A-T, B-T, C-F, D-F, E-T
4) A-T, B-T, C-T, D-T, E-T
5) A-T, B-T, C-T, D-T, E-T
6) A-T, B-T, C-T, D-T, E-F
7) A-T, B-F, C-T, D-T, E-T
8) A-T, B-T, C-T, D-T, E-T
9) A-T, B-T, C-T, D-T, E-F
10) A-T, B-F, C-F, D-T, E-F

References and Notes

Many articles, books, and websites were consulted for this work. The Quran is the primary source recommended to read and reflect on. Translations of the meanings of the Quran are found everywhere (e.g. iQuran) However, the Message of the Quran, translated and explained by the Austrian writer, Leopold Weiss (Muhammad Assad) is used as a guide. (43)

1. **Mahmoud, Mustafa.** *What is Islam?* Cairo : Dar Al-Marif, 1996. ISBN 977-02-5282-4.

2. **Sarwar, Shykh Muhammad and Toropov., Brandon.** *The Complete Idiot's Guide to Understanding Koran.* s.l. : Beach Brook Productions , 2003. 2003. ISBN 1-59257-105-0 .

3. **Mahran, Khalid.** Interfaith Ten commandments. *www.quranforall.info.* [Online] Rosetta Softmedia, 2010.

4. **Usmani, Mufti Muhammad Taqi.** *Translation of The Meanings of The Noble Quran with explanatory notes.* Karachi, Pakistan : Maktaba Ma'ariful Quran, 2006. ISBN 978-9695640005.

5. Tests show UK Quran manuscript is among world's oldest. *www.cnn.com.* [Online] CNN, July 22, 2015. [Cited:

August 6, 2016.] www.cnn.com/2015/07/22/europe/uk-quran-birmingham....

6. **Bucaille, Maurice.** *The Bible, the Quran and Science: The Holy Scriptures Examined in the Light of Modern Knowledge.* 2003. ISBN 978-1879402980.

7. **Alban, Deane.** The Brain Benefits of Learning a Second Language. *Be Brain Fit.* [Online] 2012. [Cited: August 7, 2016.] http://bebrainfit.com/brain-benefits-learning-second-language/.

8. **Elakad, Abbas.** *Thinking is an Islamic Commandment.* Cairo : Nahdet Misr, 2003. ISBN 977-14-2400-9.

9. **Brown, Laurence.** The Big Questions: Who Made Me and Why am I Here? *YouTube.* [Online] Digital Mimbar, June 2012. [Cited: August 3, 2016.] http://youtu.be/rxNYmu1yIh4.

10. **Lang, Jeffery.** *Even Angels Ask: A Journey to Islam in America.* Beltsville : Amana Publications; 1st edition, 1997. ISBN 978-0915957675.

11. **Lang, Jeffry.** purpose of Life. *YouTube.* [Online] Islam on Demand, February 27, 2011. [Cited: August 7, 2016.] http://youtu.be/ifllgTA2pmY.

12. **Parsons, John.** Name of God/Scripture/Shema. *Hebrew for Christians.* [Online] Hebrew4christians.com. [Cited: August 3, 2106.] Hebrew4christians.com.

13. **Armstrong, Karen.** *Muhammad: A Prophet for Our Time.* New York : HarperCollins, 2007. ISBN 978-0-06-115577-2.

14. **Hart, Michael.** *The 100: A Ranking Of The Most Influential Persons In History.* New York : Kensington, 2000. ISBN 0-8065-1350-0.

15. **Carlyle, Thomas.** *Heroes and Hero Worship.* s.l. : BOOK JUNGLE , 2007. ISBN 9781604241884.

16. **Rauf, Feisal Abdul.** *What's Right with Islam: A New Vision for Muslims and the West.* New York : HarperCollins, 2004. ISBN 0-06-075062-6.

17. **Bruce Bickel, Stan Jantz.** *Bible Prophecy 101.* s.l. : Harvest House Publisher, 2004. ISBN 9780736913287.

18. **Brown, Lawrence.** *The First and final commandment.* s.l. : Amana Publication, 2004. ISBN 1-59008-028-9.

19. **Ehrman, Bart.** How Jesus became God. *YouTube.* [Online] American Humanist Association , May 14, 2014. [Cited: August 7, 2016.] https://youtu.be/B5-MoJvGZVI.

20. —. *How Jesus Became God: The Exaltation of a Jewish Preacher from Galilee.* s.l. : HarperOne; Reprint edition , 2015. ISBN 978-0061778193.

21. —. Misquoting Jesus. *YouTube.* [Online] lecture at The Cathedral College of Washington National Cathedral ,

August 6, 2014. [Cited: August 7, 2016.] https://youtu.be/Pz-z8j67Ids.

22. —. *Misquoting Jesus: The Story Behind Who Changed the Bible and Why.* s.l. : HarperOne, 2007. ISBN 978-0060859510.

23. *Holy Bible, New Living Translation.* s.l. : Tyndale House Foundation, 2015.

24. **Brown, Dan.** *The Da Vinci Code.* s.l. : Random House, Inc., 2003. ISBN 978-0-307-47427-8.

25. **Johnson, Timothy.** *Finding God in the Questions: A Personal Journey.* s.l. : IVP Books , 2006. ISBN 978-0830833474.

26. **Waris Maqsood, Ruqaiyyah.** *What Every Christian Should Know About Islam.* Markfield, United Kingdom : Islamic Foundation, 2009. ISBN 9780860373759 .

27. **Emerick, Yahiya.** *The Complete Idiot's Guide to Islam.* Indianapolis : Alpha, 2002. ISBN 0-02-864233-3.

28. **Hathout, Maher.** *In Pursuit Of Justice.* Los Angeles, California : Muslim Public Affairs Council, 2006. ISBN 0-9774404-051295.

29. **Hathout, Hassan.** *Reading the Muslim Mind.* s.l. : American Trust Publications; 7th Edition edition , 2005. ISBN 978-0892591572.

30. **Wolf, Michael.** The Hajj One American's Pilgrimage To Mecca Friday, April 18, 1997 ABC News. *TouTube.* [Online] ABC NEWS, December 4, 2013. [Cited: Februrary 16, 2016.] http://youtu.be/Y6wAn-9pzpw.

31. **Elghazali, Mohamed.** *Human Rights; Teachings of Islam and UN Declaration.* Cairo : Nahdet Misr, 2003. ISBN 977-14-2400-9.

32. **The Gideons.** *The Holy Bible, King James Version.* Nashville : National Publishing Company, 1978. ISBN 0-8340-0425-9.

33. **Bales, Kevin.** *Ending Slavery.* s.l. : University of California Press, 2008. ISBN 978-0-520-25470-1.

34. **Mangera, Nazim.** *100 Inspirational Sayings of Prophet Muhammed.* 2012. ISBN 978-0-988-3174-1-3.

35. **Ali, Nancy.** From (Catholic) Church To Christ. *YouTube.* [Online] January 28, 2012. [Cited: Februrary 17, 2016.] http://youtu.be/6g_vwCMRFzk.

36. **Esposito, John.** *What everyone needs to know about Islam* . New York : Oxford University Press, Inc. SECOND EDITION, 2011. ISBN 978-0-19-979423-2 (ebook).

37. **Gore, Al.** *The Assault on Reason.* s.l. : Penguin, 2007 . ISBN 1-59420-122-6.

38. **Leupp, Gary.** Challenging Ignorance on Islam: a Ten-Point Primer for Americans. [Online] [Cited: August 7,

2016.]
http://www.muslimpopulation.com/America/USA/Challenge.php.

39. **Sheikh, Zia U. PhD.** *Islam: Silencing the Critics, 2nd ed.* 2012. ISBN 978-1470150402.

40. **Siddiqui, Haroon.** *Being a Muslim.* Canada 2006 : s.n., 2006. ISBN-10: 0-88899-786-8.

41. **Ciment, James.** *Social Issues in America: An Encyclopedia.* New York : Routledge, 2015. ISBN 9780765680617.

42. **Ibn-Hanbal, Ahmed.** *Musned: A collection of Prophet Muhammad Traditions.*

43. **Asad, Muhammed.** *The Message of the Quran.* Gibraltar : New Era Pubns , 1980. ISBN 978-0317524567.

CPSIA information can be obtained
at www.ICGtesting.com
Printed in the USA
FSOW01n1104050217
30412FS